THE EUROPEAN COMMUNITY: THE SOCIAL DIMENSION

About the Issues in Human Resource Management Series

This series of monographs is the medium by which the Human Resource Research Centre at Cranfield School of Management publishes the research findings which have emanated from its research projects. The primary aims of the Centre are to provide research expertise in order to investigate human resource issues and to assist in an appropriate, practical way with the solution of management problems. As a consequence the Centre extends the quality and quantity of research in the management of human resources and publishes this series on relevant theoretical and scientific issues. It is intended for the thinking practitioner as much as for the academic, for the consultant in human resources as much as for the student learning about these problems for the first time.

Series titles published by the Cranfield School of Management and available from Kogan Page:

1. *The 'N' Factor in Executive Survival* by Shaun Tyson, Christine Barclay and John Handyside.
2. *The Management of Expatriates* by Chris Brewster.
3. *Employee Relations Developments in the Electronics Industry* by Patricia Summers and Chris Brewster.

THE EUROPEAN COMMUNITY: THE SOCIAL DIMENSION

Labour Market Policies for 1992

Paul Teague

Issues in Human Resource Management
Series Editor: Shaun Tyson

Monograph 4

KOGAN PAGE

Published in association with the
CRANFIELD SCHOOL OF MANAGEMENT

First published in 1989 by
Kogan Page Ltd,
120 Pentonville Rd, London N1 9JN
in association with the Cranfield School of Management,
Cranfield Institute of Technology, Cranfield, Bedford MK43 0AL.

Typeset by J&L Composition Ltd, Filey, North Yorkshire
Printed and bound in Great Britain by
Biddles Ltd, Guildford and King's Lynn

British Library Cataloguing in Publication Data
Teague, Paul
The European Community: the social dimension: labour market policies for 1992. — (Issues in human resource management: no. 4).
1. European Economic Community. Social policies
I. Title II. Series
361.6′1′094
ISBN 07494–0031–5

Human Resource Issues in Management

Shaun Tyson, Professor of Human Resource Management

Professor Tyson, whose background is in the Social Sciences, spent 11 years as a Personnel Manager in industry before commencing a teaching career. He has acted as consultant to a variety of organisations and has managed large research projects in the UK and abroad. He has written a number of books and articles on personnel management.

Acknowledgements

I would like to thank Shaun Tyson, Chris Brewster, John Grahl, David Metcalf, Ben Roberts, and John Kelly for comments on parts of the manuscript. I am also indebted to Sarah Bury at Kogan Page for being very helpful in her editorial suggestions and improvements.

Contents

Preface

The programme to complete the internal market by 1992 has triggered a wave of Europeanisation inside the Community. In many respects the commercial world has been at the forefront of this renewed phase of integration. Companies already established on a Community scale are now upgrading and reformulating their European corporate strategies. Other businesses which have been operating on a purely domestic basis are now eyeing up opportunities in different member states. Several key economic sectors, most notably financial services, have been the scene where frantic merger and acquisition activity have taken place, and this is radically reshaping parts of the European business landscape. Obviously these developments are creating new challenges for personnel managers at the corporate level.

What is of equal importance as these new challenges is the question of whether changes will occur to national industrial relations frameworks as a result of the internal market programme. This issue has become important because powerful political actors inside the Community – the European Parliament, some member states (most notably France), the European trade unions and the President of the Commission, Jacques Delors – have argued that a social dimension needs to accompany the main market liberalising initiatives. Included in a social dimension would be legislation on health and safety, equal opportunities, part-time work, temporary workers etc.; initiatives on participation, and working time arrangements; and labour market policy measures on such matters as training and employment generation schemes. In a fully blown form, the social dimension could result in the creation of a European industrial relations framework standing above, but at the same time interacting with, the national systems already in place.

PREFACE

The possibility of established industrial relations systems being rearranged by Community-level initiatives has generated considerable worries and anxieties. So far no serious analysis has been done of the likelihood of a fully fledged social dimension being implemented in the context of 1992. This has only served to fuel speculation and fears. This monograph examines in depth the debate about the direction of Community labour market policy in the run up to and after 1992. It is hoped it will give the personnel profession and public policy makers, as well as the academic community, an informed guide to the current controversies on the issue. To guide the reader to further reading on specific topics, the monograph is comprehensively documented with references. In addition, a number of important appendices are included to furnish the reader with detailed information which allows for a fuller understanding of some points.

Introduction

During the 1970s and early 1980s the European Community was in the doldrums. A bloated agricultural sector and the seemingly insoluble problem of Britain's budgetary contributions had brought European integration to a virtual standstill. Not only were the member states unable to agree to any new political or economic initiatives, but frequently their meetings ended in much discord and acrimony. Television pictures of a disgruntled Mitterrand or Kohl and a defiant Thatcher gave the impression to the European public that the Community was on the brink of total collapse — an impression which was not far from the reality.

In recent years, however, the Community has undergone a total transformation. For it has changed from being a body with an uncertain future to one which may have a determining influence on the shape of political and economic affairs in Europe in forthcoming years. Unquestionably, the 1992 project, or more formally, the programme to complete the European internal market, has been responsible for this upturn in the fortunes of the Community.

The heart of the internal market programme consists of 300 specific proposals to remove the remaining physical, fiscal and technical barriers to trade between the member states. The concept of creating a Europe without frontiers is enthusiastically supported by all the member governments. The consensus view appears to be that market completion may trigger a virtuous circle of economic growth similar to the one enjoyed by the Common Market in its formative years.

Whether all 300 proposals will be adopted by the European Council (the supreme decision-making body of the Community) by 1992 and whether the benefits claimed from the programme will actually arise is open to question. Nevertheless, good grounds exist for regarding the 1992 project as a landmark in Community affairs. Within European, indeed world, business the project has made its mark by inducing a wave of international mergers and takeovers which otherwise might not have occurred. And among political and administrative élites, business organisations and trade unions in the various member states, the 1992 project is now seen as creating an unprecedented range of opportunities for them to exploit. In short, there appears to be a strong movement towards greater European economic and political integration.

Yet lurking beneath the surface of this picture of a resurgence in Europeanisation lie a number of disagreements which could drastically hold up the implementation of the programme, if not undermine it altogether. For instance, there is a difference of opinion between the Commission and the British Government concerning 1992 being a purely commercial project or also having a political dimension. Perhaps of more immediate concern, however, is that as the magical date draws closer divisions are beginning to emerge about the extent to which a completely liberalised internal market will require a new range of regulatory policies and institutions at the European level.

Thus there are disagreements regarding the Commission's Competition Directorate requiring stronger powers to supervise more thoroughly the growing number of transnational mergers. A difference of opinion also exists over the need to establish a European Central Bank to offset any potentially distorting effects from freeing capital markets. So, while there may be a widespread, almost universal, commitment to the ideals of the internal market programme, the indications are that its realisation will not be trouble free.

A controversy of equal, if not greater, importance surrounds a 'social dimension' in the liberalised internal market. By this is meant whether the Community should adopt positive policies and legislation on workers' rights and conditions (health and safety issues, information and consultation rights, working time arrangements, training, employment creation schemes, etc) so that these are not adversely affected, at least not to any significant extent, by the central programme of establishing open markets in Europe.

The potential for conflict on this issue is enormous. Past

attempts mainly by the Commission to establish interventionist social policies caused major divisions between some member states and Community institutions as well as between the social partners (the trade union and the employer organisations) and there are no good reasons for thinking that such hostilities would not re-occur. In fact, as many see the battle for economic revival in Europe being won or lost on the issue of labour market reform, particularly as regards the removal of purported inflexibilities (Lindbeck 1985, Giersch 1987). Any proposals from the Commission for extending present Community labour legislation would more than likely be greeted with considerable opposition.

Although there is an increasing amount of literature on the Community's monetary and competition policies in the context of 1992, virtually nothing has been written on the social dimension question. This is a glaring deficiency for the social policy issue may well turn out to be the Achilles heel of the entire project. This monograph attempts to fill this gap by assessing the extent to which a social dimension will be grafted on to the Community's internal market programme. The approach adopted is to focus on the labour market and employment fields, which have already been the subject of some type of Community action.

Five policy areas in particular are examined: the free movement of workers; cooperation between national labour market institutions; the European Social Fund; employment and labour legislation; and European collective bargaining. In each policy area a brief survey is given of the current form and extent of the Community's presence as well as an analysis of the possible developments in the context of 1992. The merit of this approach is that by focusing on concrete past and present developments the discussion will avoid the main dangers common on this issue of being abstract and/or polemical. The conclusion brings together the arguments made in each policy section and makes an informed assessment of what we can expect in the social policy field in 1992.

Chapter 1
The Free Movement of Workers

Introduction

To the architects of the Common Market, encouraging labour mobility was part of the general project of establishing a barrier-free Europe. However, initiatives in this area have met with limited success. By 1968, the member states had removed from their statutes any laws which discriminated in terms of employment against citizens of other Community countries. Yet the actual number of people taking the opportunity to work in another member state remains low.

Tables 1 and 2 indicate the situation for 1985. Table 1 details the number of workers from one member state in another Community country and the number of workers from non-member countries working in a Community state. If the figures for Belgium and Luxembourg are excluded (since these will have been distorted by the presence of Community institutions in those countries) then, with the exception of Ireland and Spain, nationals from non-EC countries account for a significantly higher percentage of foreign workers in the member states than EC nationals.

This situation suggests that the Community's efforts to promote the free movement of workers are still marginal when set against the largely historically and culturally determined patterns of immigration and emigration among the different member states.

The figures in Table 2 tend to reinforce this conclusion. For example, in 1985 268,000 Irish people emigrated to England — a traditional emigration location — as against 1,300 to West Germany, the richest member state, where the possibility of obtaining a better paid and more skilled job may have been greater. Similarly, Portuguese migrants tended to favour Germany and France for essentially culturally and historically

Table 1 **Foreign employees in the Community**

	Belgium	Denmark	Germany (FR)	Greece	France	Rep. of Ireland	Italy	Luxem-bourg	Nether-lands	Portugal	Spain	United Kingdom
Total residents (1985)												
• from Member States	584	25	1357	27(4)	1578(2)	67(4)	nd	89(1)	173	21	134(4)	729
• total foreigners	898	108	4380	87(4)	3680(4)	88(4)	211(1)	96(1)	559	80	227(4)	1700
• percentage of EEC nationals	65.0	24.1	1.0	31.0	42.9	76.1	—	92.7	30.9	26.3	59.0	42.9
Employees 1980												
• from Member States	159	11(1)	732	5	653(1)	nd	nd	nd	84	nd	nd	466(1)
• total foreigners	213	39(1)	2041	25	1208(1)	nd	nd	nd	190	26(1)	61(1)	833(1)
Employees 1985												
• from Member States	144(4)	12	520	6	640	17	14(3)	50	76	nd	nd	398
• total foreigners	191(4)	39	1555	24	1260	20	57(3)	53	166	nd	nd	821
• percentage of EEC nationals	75.4	30.6	33.4	25.0	50.8	85.0	24.6	94.3	45.8	—	—	48.5
• percentage of EEC nationals in total of employees	5.0	0.5	2.4	0.4	3.6	2.1	0.01	35.7	1.7	nd	nd	1.9

Source: Eurostat.
(1) 1981. (2) 1982. (3) 1983. (4) 1984.

Table 2 **Migrations of employees within the Community (1985)**

Origin	Belgium	Denmark	Germany (FR)	Greece	France	Rep. of Ireland	Italy	Luxem-bourg	Nether-lands	Portugal	Spain	United Kingdom
Belgium		0.1	7.8	0.1	12.5	0.1		8.5	21.3			3.3
Denmark		–	2.8	0.0	1.1	0.2		0.1	0.4			3.2
Germany (FR)		3.7	–	1.2	15.4	0.5		5.0	16.3			17.6
Greece		0.2	103.4	–	1.0	–		0.0	1.6			7.3
France		0.7	40.9	0.8	–	0.3		10.4	2.5			16.8
Rep. of Ireland		0.4	1.3	0.0	0.7	–		0.0	0.9			268.0
Italy		0.8	199.9	1.1	94.1	0.3		8.2	7.2			56.5
Luxembourg		0.0	1.1	–	–	–		–	0.1			–
Netherlands		0.8	30.3	0.2	2.7	0.4		0.8	–			9.0
Portugal		0.1	35.2	0.0	98.3	–		15.3	7.8			2.0
Spain		0.4	67.2	0.0	400.1	0.2		0.9	3.2			14.5
United Kingdom		4.4	30.0	2.7	13.4	14.7		0.5	14.9			–
Total	144	12	520	6	640	17		50	76			398
Non-Community States		27.7	1035.5	17.9	619.6	3.6		2.6	89.6			422.6

Source: Eurostat.

determined reasons. So the policy or Treaty objective of establishing a labour market inside the Community, similar to the one that exists in the United States where people are prepared to move across states if they see it to be in their professional or employment interests, has yet to be realised. Yet some inter-Community labour migration has occurred and is worth reviewing.

The Pattern of Migratory Movement

In the 1960s and early 1970s the major migratory movements were of a traditional kind, with surplus labour moving from the less developed parts of the Community to richer member states, particularly from southern Italy to West Germany. But, since the mid 1970s, with most member states experiencing a slowdown in economic growth and increases in unemployment, this form of migration has more or less dried up. Figures from the European statistical office in Luxembourg indicate that the number of Community foreign employees in member states did not vary significantly between 1980 and 1985.

However, a recent report by the Commission on labour mobility inside the Community suggests that, 'traditional forms of migration are increasingly giving way to "fluid exchanges" of skilled persons moving about all over the community without constituting particularly significant net migratory movements.' (Commission of the EC 1988 p 10.) By and large this type of labour mobility is the result of transnational companies moving their staff across different geographical (national) sites inside the Community. In other words, if the Commission's report is accurate, transnationals are compensating for shortcomings in the Community labour market, such as the lack of free movement of workers or skill shortages in specific regions, by developing their own EC-wide internal labour markets. The significant point to grasp about this form of cross-national labour mobility is that it surmounts the various cultural and practical barriers associated with traditional forms of migration. Given that a substantial proportion of Community trade involves transnationals in intra-trade and intra-service movements, and given that mergers among companies in the various member states are increasing, it is highly likely that this more fluid form of labour mobility will become more widespread.

From an official Community point of view, such a development should be welcomed, for it makes up for some of the inadequacies of not having a truly open EC labour market. Although it is recognised that 'fluid migration' does bring benefits and is probably now a permanent feature of the European labour market, the Community is still eager to implement fully the long-standing Treaty objective of free movement of workers. For 1992, therefore, a major programme is planned to reduce some of the remaining barriers to labour mobility between the member states.

Measures to Increase the Free Movement of Workers

Upgrading the legal instruments

There are a number of aspects of this programme to create, in Commission terminology, a true vocational and occupational area inside the Community. One aspect is the reformulation and strengthening of existing legislation which guarantees workers and their families geographical and occupational mobility as well as social integration. Although Community legislation prohibits member states from discriminating against workers from other member states, many cases of unequal treatment have arisen in this area. Such inequality has occurred partly because member states have not fully or properly incorporated the relevant Community legislation into national law, and partly because in developing new statutes and policies they have not taken full account of restrictions imposed by the Community (Brewster and Teague, 1989 Chapter 7).

Table 3 on pages 20–1 gives examples of legislation, regulations and administrative practices of some member states which were found to be incompatible with the rules of the freedom of movement.

To close this gap between Community legal provision and actual national practice, the Commission proposes for 1992

Table 3 **Examples of legislation, regulations, circulars and administrative practices of the member states adopted since 1968 and regarded as incompatible with the rules of freedom of movement**

this list is illustrative and not of course exhaustive. Most of the cases listed below have been resolved.

Belgium

- Legislation with respect to additional registration fees for foreigners required EEC workers and members of their families to pay foreign student fees, contrary to Articles 7 and 12 of Regulation 1612/68 establishing equal treatment with respect to access to vocational training and general education.
- Certain provisions relating to the grant of various types of social assistance discriminated against EEC workers and members of their families.
- Additional leave for mineworkers was not granted to EEC workers doing their military service in their country of origin.

Federal Republic of Germany

- The law denied access to the profession of doctor in an employed capacity to the non-EEC spouse of an EEC worker.
- The law took no account of military service performed in the country of origin of an EEC worker.
- The administrative practice in certain Lánder permitted the expulsion of EEC workers or former EEC workers exercising their right of residence because they had applied for social assistance.
- Certain regional laws limit the grant of parental leave to bring up a child to German nationals.
- German income tax law makes no provision for rebates in the case of an EEC worker's dependent children living abroad.

France

- The Maritime Code excluded EEC workers from access to employment as seamen.
- The Labour Code prohibited temporary employment businesses from recruiting EEC workers for duties outside France.
- The Family Code and Social Assistance did not provide for the issue of a national priority card for pregnant women to Community workers and spouses of EEC workers.
- The Health Code restricted access to permanent employment as nurses in public hospitals to French nationals.
- A decision by the City Council of Paris restricted the grant of parental leave for bringing up a child to parents of French nationality.
- A Ministry of Education circular submitted the award of university study grants to conditions which discriminated against these workers and their children.

Italy

- The law excluded EEC workers from ownership of State-subsidised housing.

- Certain regional laws restricted access to the occupation of ski instructor to Italians.
- Certain forms of vocational training were reserved for Italians.
- Access to the occupation of frogman was restricted to Italians.
- The law prevented EEC research workers from occupying permanent posts on the staff of the National Research Council.

Luxembourg

- The law prohibited the grant of certain social advantages to nationals of member states who did not meet the condition of a period of residence in Luxembourg.
- In Luxembourg, genuine equal treatment is not ensured for children of EEC workers as regards access to education, for it excludes the latter from its bilateral agreements with Belgium on education.

Netherlands

- The law banned access to certain social advantages by EEC workers working part-time. Similarly, the authorities prohibited the exercise of the right of freedom of movement to EEC workers planning to work part-time.
- The authorities did not apply to EEC workers a provision allowing family reunion with the spouse.

United Kingdom

- Administrative practice with respect to access to State-subsidised housing discriminated against Community workers.
- Regulations with regard to the award of study grants included conditions which discriminated against EEC workers and their children.

---

to update and extend regulation 1612/68, which was the Community legislation removing all legal barriers to labour mobility between member states. In addition, it plans to undertake what can best be described as a 'legal audit' of the member states to ensure that their existing laws and practices in the area coincide with Community legislation. These actions may remove the remaining legal loopholes which have so far prevented a comprehensive statutory programme for free movement of workers being implemented by each member state. It is questionable, however, whether such a programme, by itself, will lead to a quantitative increase in mobility inside the Community. The Commission appears to accept this to be the case for, in addition to these actions in the legislative field, it has proposed a number of other initiatives (interviews with Commission officials).

Obtaining the mutual recognition of diplomas and training qualifications

Another major obstacle identified as preventing the free movement of workers is the lack of and, in many instances, the non-recognition of training qualifications and professional diplomas across the member states. Thus, in the immediate future the Commission intends to launch a new range of measures to obtain greater mutual recognition of training, professional and educational qualifications.

To some extent this is not a new policy. In 1974 the Council adopted a resolution laying down that training and professional qualifications should be harmonised inside the Community. But when the Commission came to draw up specific policy proposals on this resolution it realised almost immediately that such a task would be virtually impossible. As a result, the Council lowered its sights and the less ambitious approach was adopted of getting the Commission to propose Directives listing each member state's diploma awards for specific professions which would be recognised in all the EC countries. This revised approach met with some success as five Directives have now been passed by the Council, covering doctors, nurses, vets, dentists and midwives.

In what can be regarded as a follow-up initiative, the Council adopted a resolution in 1985 on the compatibility of vocational training qualifications. It aimed to enable workers to make better use of their qualifications, particularly as regards to them obtaining suitable employment in another member state. Among other things, the resolution obliged the Commission to establish a steering committee made up of representatives from the labour market institutions of various member states and the social partners to supervise the initiative.

The first initiative undertaken by this group in conjunction with the European Centre for the Development of Vocational Training (CEDEFOP) was to devise a structure of training levels so that Community action to obtain greater mutual recognition would be able to tackle the problems of individual occupational sectors and professional and diploma awards.

A five-tier training structure along the following lines was established:

Level I: Compulsory education and professional training.
This level of training is relatively low. The volume of theoretical knowledge and practical capabilities involved is very limited. Normally, this form of training enables the holder to perform relatively simple work and may be quickly acquired.

Level II: Compulsory education and vocational training.
This level covers the situation where the worker is fully qualified to engage in a specific activity, chiefly involving tasks which may be independent within the boundaries of specifically defined work arrangements.

Level III: Compulsory education and/or vocational training and additional technical training or technical education training or other secondary level training.
This form of training involves a greater amount of theoretical knowledge than Level II. Activity involves mainly technical work which can be performed independently and/or entail executive and coordination duties.

Level IV: Secondary training (general or vocational) and post-secondary training.
This level involves high-level technical training and gives the worker the capabilities and knowledge to work in a generally independent way and to assume design and/or management and/or administrative responsibilities.

Level V: Secondary training and complete higher education.
This form of training involves occupations where the mastery of scientific knowledge is required and which involves high autonomous forms of work.

As a first step towards obtaining greater comparability of vocational training qualifications, the working party selected a group of occupations from the lower training levels to form a pilot scheme on the issue. The occupational categories selected were hotel and catering, motor vehicle repair and construction. The pilot scheme was given the task of drawing up mutually agreed descriptions of the occupations and occupational requirements in force in the various categories.

The objective was to harmonise the vocational training qualifications recognised in the different member states on the basis of established descriptions. The occupations were selected because they were regarded as relatively open to the mutual recognition approach. Each national labour market institution (eg, in the UK, it was the then called Manpower Services Commission (MSC, now the Training Agency) was charged with the responsibility of investigating what revisions would be required to other member states' qualifications to make them broadly comparable with its existing national qualifications.

Work on these three sectors is now more or less complete and the Commission hopes to publish the results in the near future. In anticipation that the Council will support its recommendations on these three sectors, the Commission has started work on three further sectors; agriculture, the electrical industry and the forestry industry.

In interviews with officials from the Commission and UK government bodies, it was suggested that the difficulties and complexities of obtaining comparability of vocational training qualifications had been considerably underestimated by the working party in its early deliberations. The consensus view was that if the member states are going to make any discernible progress on this policy goal then they will have to increase substantially the number of personnel working in this area. At the moment, the ultimate objective of allowing Community citizens to take a job in their field in any member state without any non-recognition problems, appears a long way in the distance. It is clear, therefore, that a greater level of action is required if these policy objectives are going to be realised.

Modernising the relevant Community institutions

The Community also tries to encourage the free movement of labour through the European system for the international clearing of vacancies and applications for employment (SEDOC). This body was set up by Regulation No 1612/68, but did not come into effect until 1973. Its main task is to promote the exchange of information relating to unfilled national vacancies and applications at the Community level. The system is based on a register of occupations and professions open to international exchange, and it works by vacancies and applications being telexed each month by the SEDOC service in one member state to SEDOC services in the others. If this reveals the existence of a particular vacancy or application with opportunity for clearing, the system passes further detailed information. In addition to exchanging vacancies and applications for employment, SEDOC also provides information for workers willing to work in another member state and for employers unable to find the workers they require on the national market.

The general opinion is that the results procured from SEDOC since its establishment have been fairly modest. A number of administrative and technical arrangements appear to limit its effectiveness. For instance, the register for occupations was compiled between 1972–74, which means that it does not contain most of the new occupations created by recent technological developments. Despite its lack-lustre performance, the Commission intends to overhaul and update the system in the context of 1992. Four changes will occur as a result of the Commission's revitalisation programme:

(1) The system will be extended to the new member states — Spain and Portugal.
(2) The SEDOC register of occupations will be reclassified and updated.
(3) The exchange network will be computerised, allowing for the transfer of more frequent and comprehensive information.
(4) The type of information transferred will be broadened.

These changes will obviously improve the system, but against a background of high European unemployment, of the apparent reluctance of workers within the Community to cross frontiers for new jobs, and of the widespread qualitative gap between vacancies and applications for employment in the member states, it would be optimistic to hold out much hope for the SEDOC system being transformed into a truly effective Community agency.

Improving cooperation between national employment agencies
Another way in which the Commission attempts to obtain greater mobility is by improving cooperation between the various national employment services. In 1980, for instance, the Council adopted a resolution which stipulated that the Community should increase its activity on labour market policy in the following three areas:

(1) *Improvement of labour market knowledge.* In particular it was recommended that cooperation be strengthened between national and Community employment services in matters such as the length of the working week, different forms of employment, unemployment flows, etc.
(2) *Development and cooperation of placement services.* Provisions were made for an action programme for the development and cooperation between national placement services, particularly in areas such as staff training.
(3) *Concerted forward-looking management of the labour market.* The aim here was to increase cooperation between the social partners and the employment services so as to achieve forward-looking manpower utilisation policies.

It was hoped that these reforms would improve the speed and quality of information exchanges on labour market matters between the member states, thereby facilitating the free movement of workers.

To encourage cooperation between national employment services for this policy goal, the Commission has sponsored regular exchanges between officials of national employment services. It is hoped that these exchanges will smooth out specific administrative and organisational problems hindering labour mobility and will establish arrangements to ease the process of communication between different national bodies. In 1986 the Commission spent around 350,000 ECU (European Currency Units: one ECU is worth about 75 pence) on these exchanges, involving 275 officials. The exchanges normally fall into two categories. One takes the form of a one to two month traineeship, while the other is only a two-day visit.

Conclusions

To summarise then, in the context of 1992 there will be an intensification of traditional policies and the creation of new ones in an attempt to obtain genuine free labour mobility inside the Community. Obviously this new drive will pay some dividends, but it is open to question whether it will be strong enough to flatten the long-standing cultural and social barriers preventing workers from moving from one Community country to another. The evidence suggests that this policy must be regarded in a long-term objective, requiring substantial and constant policy action by national labour market institutions. At present, the scale of action required is being underestimated by the Community and national organisations. A number of the current Community schemes appear to have inadequate resources or at least could do with additional personnel. Free movement of workers will not occur spontaneously; it will involve a hard policy grind.

Chapter 2
Cooperation between National Labour Market Institutions

Introduction: Types of Cooperation Initiatives

Over the years the Community has attempted in a number of ways to obtain greater policy cooperation between the labour market and training institutions from the different member states. One way, as was shown in the last chapter, is the encouragement of regular exchange visits between officials of different national departments to foster a greater mutual understanding. The most significant benefit of these exchanges is that personal contacts and relationships are formed allowing problems involving a number of different national labour institutions to be resolved more easily. Another way used to promote cooperation has been to involve national labour market policy-makers from the different member states in Community-level discussions on certain policy areas. Thus, for example, officials from the British Health and Safety Commission sit on the Community's Advisory Committee on Safety, Hygiene and Health at Work along with representatives of similar organisations from other member states.

Theoretically, the main purpose of involving national officials in such committees is to assist the Commission in its task of devising Community-wide labour market policies and/or obtaining greater convergence in the public policies of the member states on such issues. A variety of different initiatives has emerged from these committees. One is the sponsorship of innovatory projects to encourage new and original ways to deal with certain labour market problems. So, for example, in 1986 the Advisory Committee on Vocational Training launched the Eurotechnet Project, which involved each member state committing itself to devising national pilot schemes over a three-year period on the theme of vocational training and new technology.

The purpose of each scheme was to devise new and experimental training methods and packages for the new technologies. A Community-level steering committee was set up and bilateral contacts were encouraged so that progress could be monitored and assessed and an exchange of ideas and experiences could take place. From these various national pilot schemes it was hoped that new and better training techniques would emerge, thereby giving people in every member state the opportunity to master more effectively new technological equipment and processes.

Synchronisation Schemes: Youth Training as an Example

Another type of initiative relating to labour market and training questions launched by Community committees may be called synchronisation schemes. Here the objective is to bring about convergence of public policies of member states on labour market issues. A good recent example is the attempt to obtain a more synchronised approach to youth training. In 1983 the Council adopted a resolution stipulating that member states

> 'will do their utmost so that all young people who so wish . . . can benefit over a period of at least six months and if possible one year following full-time compulsory education from a full-time programme involving basic training and/or an initial work experience to prepare them for an occupation . . . moreover, will pursue their efforts, in the context of their national policies and practices, to see that young people without sufficient qualifications, including particularly those who are looking for work, have adequate opportunities for vocational training to improve their skills and qualifications' (Commission of the EC 1987a, p 13).

In other words, the Council resolution was stipulating that a Community-wide *social guarantee* should be established for young people as regards to training.

The Commission was given the task of coordinating action towards this goal. In 1983 it produced a comparative analysis of youth training in the member states to assess how far the Community had moved toward establishing a social guarantee. The conclusion of the Commission's analysis was that most member states had met or would soon meet the minimum commitment to offer some basic vocational training to all young people after they had finished compulsory schooling.

But the Commissions analysis also made clear that apart from establishing a basic level of training provision, important distinctions in training, vocational and educational structures continue to exist among the member states. At one end of the spectrum, some members combine vocational training and work experience (eg Germany and Denmark). At the other end, some member states, most notably France, have full-time vocational education within the formal educational system. In between are the countries like the UK which have a mixture of the two systems.

The diverse systems have given rise to different forms of training and qualifications that hinder the free movement of workers. They also cause the quality of training to differ significantly between the member states. The Commission is aware of these shortcomings for, having established what it terms a social guarantee — in other words the offer of some type of training for every young person leaving school in the Community — it is now proposing that member states concentrate on obtaining greater convergence in the quality and distribution of youth education and training.

Labour Market Cooperation and 1992: Potential and Limitations

The objective of achieving more convergence of member states' labour market policies will, in all likelihood, be at the centre of the Community's cooperation initiatives up to and beyond 1992. The extent to which schemes of this type will be successful largely depends on the degree of symmetry that already exists in the respective policy areas: the greater the degree of divergence the less successful Community synchronisation initiatives will be. This is simply because more extensive reorganisation of national practices would be required to meet the Community norm. The standard practice of most national policy-makers participating in Community committees is to avoid agreeing to any synchronised initiatives that would entail large scale alteration of existing national practice. Such an approach was aptly summed up by an official of the British Health and Safety Commission when he said:

> where proposals relate to areas in which the UK has adequate domestic legislation, the objective in negotiations is to ensure that the final EC instrument is, as far as possible, consistent with our legislation. This was the case with the proposal for the Directive on the protection of workers from lead (UK). Regulations on this subject were made a year before the Directive was adapted and it was not necessary to amend them as a result of the Directive. Only minor changes to the accompanying Approved Code of Practice were necessary (Health and Safety Executive 1987).

To illustrate the extent to which the Commission may be able to harmonise policy between the member states, the degree of convergence or divergence in three labour market areas within the Community is examined below.

Health and safety

Approaches to occupational health and safety in the member states reveal a surprising degree of diversity. Apart from Britain, only Denmark has opted for a unified government organisation which is wholly and exclusively responsible for policy and administration in the area of health and safety. Other countries' systems reflect differing federal structures, a broader definition of the role of labour inspection, or a distinction between health inspection and safety inspection.

These differences in organisation make direct comparisons between countries extremely difficult. The problems of comparison may be best illustrated by considering the occupational and health and safety systems in two of the largest EC member states, France and Germany, and comparing them with the British health and safety arrangements.

France

The French system is complex, comprising a number of government agencies with different but partially overlapping responsibilities. The largest element is formed by *Services Extérieures du Travail et de l'Emploi* (SETE), part of the Ministry of Social Affairs. SETE is responsible for the inspection of employed people (as opposed to the self-employed) in most of industry and commerce. However, the responsibilities of the SETE inspectors go much further than those of the British Health and Safety Executive (HSE). In addition to health and safety, they cover conditions of work and many industrial relations activities including conciliation and arbitration in disputes and the sanctioning of collective dismissals on economic grounds.

The role of French inspectors, therefore, is fundamentally different from that of the HSE's field staff. The French inspectors spend the major part of their time on labour relations matters. It has been estimated that health and safety may take up only 15 to 20 per cent of their time. An additional difference between France and Britain is that most inspectoral effort is devoted to investigating accidents and complaints, leaving little scope for preventive inspection. French inspectors see their health and safety role as primarily concerned with enforcing the law.

Germany

In West Germany there is a dual system of inspection. Each of the 11 Lander has an inspectorate responsible for enforcing industrial safety legislation in a wide range of industries. These inspectorates, or *Gewerbeaufsicht* (GAs), are principally concerned with the prevention of accidents and ill health, including the enforcement of federal and state legislation, social conditions such as hours of work and, in most states, environmental protection.

The second part of the system is the network of mutual insurance bodies, or *Berufsgenossenschaften* (BGs). There are 95 BGs covering specific sectors although some are also regionally based. They are financed by employers' contributions and managed jointly by employers and employees, but their existence is based on law and overall supervision is exercised by the Federal Ministry of Labour. The BGs can draw up accident prevention regulations which, after approval by the Federal Ministry, may be formally adopted and published. On publication they become legally binding on firms covered by the relevant BG.

Germany is the only member state that gives such a prominent role to insurance in the setting and enforcement of occupational health and safety standards. One direct consequence of the regulatory powers of the BGs is that the volume of health and safety legislation is much greater and more detailed than it is in Britain. Both the GA and BG inspectors spend much of their time on visits in response to complaints, or requests for advice, especially in the case of the BG's reported accidents. Both have powers to issue administrative fines for minor offences, to issue notices and ultimately to ask the public prosecutor's office to pursue offenders through the courts.

As will be made clear later on, health and safety is the only area which indisputably comes under the qualified majority voting system introduced by the Single European Act. Thus, there is every possibility that this area will become an increasingly important aspect of Community policies on employment conditions.

This brief review suggests that the Community will have considerable difficulty in establishing a uniform system or the machinery for implementing health and safety legislation across the member states, or in getting agreement if this involves changing the existing institutional arrangements for implementing policies. So efforts towards agreement in the health and safety fields should concentrate mainly on standards to be implemented within the diverse institutions.

Social security

Member states are now facing similar problems in the area of social security:

- The increasing numbers of the elderly as a proportion of the population, has put a strain on the operation and financing of social security systems.
- The need to fund persistent and historically high unemployment is faced by all the member states.

- As many European social security systems were established before single parenthood existed on anything like its present scale, most member states are facing increasing demands from this and other sections of what is termed the 'new poor' or the 'new under class'.

In combination, these problems mean that the operation and financing of social security systems will be a major problem in all member states. Given that the issues of concern appear to be broadly similar across the Community, is there a possibility of cooperation between the member states in this area?

The evidence suggests that formidable barriers to the complete harmonisation of social security provision exist within the Community. To begin with, social security provisions are based on different assumptions in the different member states. Take, for instance, the system of family benefits in France and Great Britain. A major difference exists in the structure of family benefits, varying with family size and the age of the children. In France no benefit is paid for the first child, and in the case of a two-child family, there is no premium for the elder child. This means that one-child, and to a lesser extent, two-child families in Britain are definitely better off. On the other hand, in France there is a higher additional amount for the third and subsequent children so that the level of assistance rises from 32 per cent of the base amount for the two-child family to 73 per cent of the base amount for the three-child family and then by a further 41 per cent for each additional child. Thus, there is a strong 'tilt' in favour of larger families in France. Significant differences also occur in other aspects of the social security provisions in France and Britain. This is a two-country comparison on one issue only. Multiplied, it indicates the scale of problems that would arise if setting common social protection standards becomes a Community objective.

A second difficulty lies in the administrative and organisational differences between the EC countries in the field of social security. Occupational pension schemes are but one example. In Great Britain and the Irish Republic, for instance, the basic state provision may be regarded as a pension which covers the fundamental requirements of life with no luxuries. But Spain, Italy and Portugal provide a state pension which is earnings-related and which provides an adequate pension related to earnings for all. Other countries would fit in between these two systems.

In addition, the British system is means tested and is the only centralised system in the EC. Other systems are, to a greater or lesser degree, localised and segmented in the sense that there are different systems for different categories of pension. This situation led the National Association of Pension Funds to comment that 'the state pension arrangements in the EEC are so different that it will be almost impossible to achieve harmonisation of benefit levels or indeed benefits themselves at least within a feasible time span' (National Association of Pension Funds 1987, p 126).

A further problem is that if social security harmonisation is taken to mean the equalisation upwards of the level of benefits then enormous burdens would be placed on the poorer member states. They would face a major increase in their financial bill in this area. Some analysts suggest that if such a policy were to be seriously considered then the richer member states would have to transfer resources to the poorer member countries.

The conclusion must be that as each European social security system has been established in a different set of historical circumstances and inherited different sets of traditions and priorities, the possibility of complete harmonisation hardly exists in the short term. This conclusion appears to be accepted by Community institutions (Commission of EC 1988), although attempts are being made to obtain a degree of partial harmonisation on specific subjects such as the portability of pensions.

Measures in favour of the long-term unemployed

Measures to bring the long-term unemployed back into the labour market have been identified by the Commission as a priority area for employment policy within member states. Although exact definitions differ, it is broadly accepted that

Table 4 The range of programmes introduced by member states for the long-term unemployed in the 1980s

	Belgium	Denmark	Germany	Spain	France	Greece
Personalised counselling			*Personalised counselling* after every three months of unemployment		Personal interviews assessment and programme after 13 months unemployment	
Fostering self-help			*FdA financial aids* for travel etc to enable LTUs to find and take up jobs			
Fostering self-employment		*Enterprise allowance scheme* to help start up own firm instead of receiving a second Job Offer	*Bridging allowance* for three months	*Reduction of interest* on loan and technical assistance grant	Helping the unemployed set up own business *Departmental youth initiative fund* for LTUs aged over 25	
Financing specialised training			*Training* to improve placement prospects. Grant for training period within an employment contract	*Basic and vocational retraining* for LTUs over 25 years (75 per cent of statutory minimum wage)	*Modular traineeships* 300 to 1200 hours for over 25 year olds *Training and reinsertion aid programme:* 550 hours training plus two months in enterprise for young people; and 300 to 700 hours for adults	
Insertion into existing training		*Training allowance* for up to two years for under 25 year olds *Training allowance* instead of second Job Offer	LTUs are encouraged to participate in existing courses only once they have come to grips with their personal and vocational situation so as to reduce the number of drop-outs	*Vocational training in rural areas*: LTUs over 25 years receive 75 per cent of minimum wage. Free VT for LTUs aged over 45 after being given indefinite employment contracts	18–25 traineeships Employment-training contracts *ANPE* upgrading *FNE* traineeships	Priority on courses to LTUs
Work contracts			Fixed-term trial employment	*Indefinite contracts* for LTUs aged over 45 Indefinite contracts for employing women aged over 45 in		

Special work programmes	*TCT-Third work circuit*: new permanent, non-market community jobs. State pays 95 per cent of wage, plus social security (1982–86) Promoting employment in the non-market sector		Public interest job creation	Priority in *collaboration* contracts of public sector bodies with INEM: maximum grant of 100 per cent	*Part-time collective utility jobs* for 16 to 21 year olds (1984) extended to 21 to 25 year olds *Part-time work for* LTUs aged over 25 years for six months	
Subsidising normal work		*Job offers* for jobs lasting at least seven months in public (nine in private) sector after two years	*Wage subsidies* for over 50 year old LTUs hired for additional jobs Loans or subsidies for organising, extending and equipping firms and departments aimed at providing work for older workers Settling in allowance Occupational trial periods	In cooperatives: loan interest reductions for LTUs Encouraging local employment initiatives for LTUs *Work experience contracts* for 25 year old with dependants	*Aids to employer* and topping up unemployment benefit for part-time employment *Financial compensation* for LTUs accepting part-time jobs at wages below unemployment benefit levels	12,000 12-month grants to firms for hiring LTUs
Fostering early retirements	*Early retirement* by collective agreement for workers aged 57 or over replaced by unemployed people	*Voluntary early retirement scheme*: replacements by LTUs are encouraged	*Early retirement scheme* enables LTUs to be hired in replacement			
Extending unemployment allowance			Extension of maximum duration of receipt of receipt of unemployment benefit over 42 years old	Over 55 year olds on unemployment assistance qualifying for retirement pension can receive 75 per cent of minimum statutory wage	LTUs of over 57 years get unemployment benefit without signing on until age 60, when they receive early retirement pension	

	Ireland	Italy	Luxemburg	Netherlands	Portugal	United Kingdom
Personalised counselling	*Direct action (pilot) programme*: integrated package of counselling, plus job or place on training programme					*Restart* offering all LTUs practical advice and help to secure jobs
Fostering self-help	*Job search scheme*: coaching in job-search techniques					*Jobclubs* providing LTUs with meeting place, coaching and material facilities
Fostering self-employment	*Enterprise scheme*: LTUs constitute 40 per cent of participants			*Start-up assistance scheme*: income supplement plus loan	*Self-employment aids* programme *Capitalised unemployment insurance scheme* for enterprise creation	*Enterprise allowance scheme*: £40 (ECU 55) a week allowance for one year to set up own business — not just LTUs
Financing specialised training	*Building on experience* for LTUs aged 25 to 44: six months alternating formal training and on-the-job training *Management development* programme for LTU managers		Vocational training or re-education, general education courses For under 25 year olds: introductory courses in companies; temporary manpower programme contracts; initiation traineeship contracts			*Restart* training course for updating basic skills and job search techniques of one week plus one day for 13 weeks
Insertion into existing training	*Special employable skills* programme *Enterprise training* programmes *Educational opportunities scheme* for over 25 year olds				Priority access to reconversion and upgrading courses of state training centres	*Wider opportunities training programme* *Job training scheme*: six months training and work experience *Training for enterprise*
Work contracts	*Part-time job allowance scheme* for LTUs having found regular part-time work of less than 24 hours a week	*Training-work contracts* for 18 to 29 year olds with 15 to 30 per cent wage subsidies (1983–86)		*Temporary work contracts* of 20–32 hours a week for young LTUs through national agency (*START*) enable employers to receive subsidy of 33 percent of youth	Grants (12 times the minimum wage) to firms giving LTUs aged over 25 open-ended employment contracts	

Special work programmes	*Social employment*: part-time work in non-profit-making organisations, paid ECU 92–112 on half-weekly basis	*Enhancing cultural assets*: finance for projects hiring additional LTUs aged under 29 on fixed-term contracts for maximum of 36 months	Aids for creating jobs of socio-economic usefulness	*Temporary jobs* for LTUs in non-profit bodies (1979–83)	Programme of temporary employment (six months) in community activities for over 25 year olds Local employment initiatives finance	*Community programme* offers jobs for up to one year of value to the community to help raise LTUs' job prospects
Subsidising normal work	*Employment incentives scheme*: subsidy to employers hiring additional workers, weighted (double premium) in favour of LTUs	Jobs in state administrations, autonomous bodies, local authorities: priority to LTUs unemployed for over six months	*Incentive premium* to hire LTUs — 200 per cent of reference minimum social wage	Employers hiring a LTU for at least six months receive up to ECU 400 a month for six months for training, etc costs *Plough back scheme:* Job creation in building, financed by unemployment benefit and public funds, 70 per cent must be LTUs *Social security exemption* for hiring LTUs unemployed over three years on indefinite contract, or a work contract for over two years, plus grant for retraining costs		*Jobstart allowance*: £20 (ECU 28) a week to LTUs who find a full-time job paying less than £80 (ECU 111) a week
Fostering early retirements					*Early retirements* for over 62 year olds (no replacement required)	*Job release scheme*: early retirers replaced by unemployed (not just LTUs) *Part-time JRS* (1983–86)
Extending unemployment allowance			Possibility of extending unemployment compensation for 182 days for particularly difficult to place unemployed people		Extended unemployment assistance for over 50 year olds	

Abbreviations: ANPE (FRANCE) — National Employment Agency
FNE (FRANCE) — National Employment Fund
FUA (GERMANY) — Incentives to enter employment.

once people have been out of work for a year or more they can be considered long-term unemployed. This group of people are believed to be distinctive for a number of reasons:

- They are seen to have fallen out of the labour market; they do not actively search for jobs, at least not to the same extent as the short to medium-term unemployed, nor do they attempt to get retrained or reskilled to enhance their employment prospects.
- They represent a large segment of the new 'under class' for whom coping with poverty has become a way of life.
- They are more vulnerable to ill-health, both physical and mental; there is a strong association between unemployment and ill-health. For such reasons, long-term unemployment is regarded by the Commission as an unacceptable social (and economic) problem.

Given that the number of specially targetted programmes for the long-term unemployed has proliferated among the member states, it would appear that most if not all of them share the Commission's anxieties on the issue. Table 4 on pp 36–9 lists the range of programmes introduced by the member states for the long-term unemployed during the 1980s. It shows that every member state has introduced some type of scheme for this group. Although the specifics of the programmes introduced may vary to some extent, there appears to be a significant degree of similarity between the member states. One common form of intervention is special work programmes: with the exception of Denmark and Greece, every Community country has introduced a scheme in this category. For the most part, special work programmes focus on creating temporary jobs, lasting six months to a year, in 'non-market' organisations (ie groups established to make environmental improvements to certain rural areas). The intention is to refamiliarise the long-term unemployed with work routines.

An equally popular method of helping the long-term unemployed appears to be subsidising normal work. Most schemes in this area offer subsidies for a limited period to employers who recruit long-term unemployed people.

To a large extent, this and the other scheme outlined above

are fairly conventional instruments used to tackle the problems of disadvantaged groups in the labour market. A more novel approach to the problem of the long-term unemployed, which is gaining increasing support across the Community, is fostering self-employment. These schemes normally take the form of offering financial assistance to those who want to start up in business. The philosophy underpinning such schemes is that instead of looking for traditional forms of employment in large factories, people should consider creating their own work.

Among the other programmes devised to address the long-term unemployed question, there are counselling sessions to restore people's confidence, self-help schemes to provide practical assistance, and training schemes to improve employment prospects and opportunities. In the sphere of employment policy, therefore, dealing with long-term unemployment, is a question where there is considerable convergence among the member states.

Conclusions

The scope for cooperative policy action for labour market and industrial relations matters varies between individual policy segments. While the possibilities for joint action on issues like the long-term unemployed appears fairly high, the degree of policy synchronisation in the social security field seems limited. This conclusion suggests that the Community needs to adopt a flexible approach to the question of policy cooperation between the member states. Although the Community will want to obtain the maximum feasible level of coordination in each policy segment, it must recognise that this level will differ across the labour market.

Chapter 3
The European Social Fund

Introduction

Since its formation, the Community has been consistently eager to directly assist employment and training initiatives as well as the economic development process more generally in the member states. One way it has done this is by establishing three European-level funds to financially assist projects and programmes:

- The *European Social Fund* primarily to sponsor employment and training initiatives.
- The *European Regional Fund* (ERDF) mainly to improve the economic infrastructure of the less advantaged regions in the Community.
- The guidance section of the *European Agricultural Guidance and Guarantee Fund* (FEOGA) to assist a range of rural development schemes such as promoting cottage industries, encouraging environmental programmes, training displaced farm workers, etc.

Together these funds are called the *European Structural Funds*.

Until recently, the Funds operated independently from each other. However, as a result of the Single European Act (see Appendix 1), the individual funds have lost their autonomy and have become integrated so as to maximise their impact within the member states. In other words, the various individual funds have now disappeared and a new entity calling the *European Structural Fund* has emerged.

The main focus of this chapter is the European Social Fund. The first part of the chapter examines the operation and impact of the Fund before the recent changes; the second part assesses how the new European Structural Fund will relate to employment and labour market matters.

The Fund during the 1970s and early 1980s

The European Social Fund is the only specific employment policy instrument established by the Treaty of Rome (Articles 123–127). For the architects of the Community, the Social Fund was seen purely as a mechanism to increase geographical and occupational mobility of workers between the member states. During the 1960s the operation of the Fund was more or less limited to that objective. But as most member states were enjoying the benefits of sustained economic growth, the number of schemes actually sponsored by the Fund were relatively few, and it was therefore regarded as a marginal part of the Community's activities.

The operation and direction of the European Social Fund changed radically in the early 1970s. In particular, the Fund underwent four major revisions, with the result that by the early 1980s it was firmly focused on helping member states combat the Community-wide unemployment problem by sponsoring employment and training schemes. No doubt the slowdown in the job creation process was the main factor behind the reorganisation of the Fund. But it should also be noted that in the 1970s the Commission was eager to shift the Fund from 'negative' to 'positive' issues and thereby help revive the faltering dynamics of European integration. Thus, instead of encouraging the free movement of workers, the Fund was assigned four new priorities:

- Tackling youth unemployment (not less than 75 per cent of total available grants were to be allocated to these projects).
- Improving employment opportunities in the Community's designated priority areas (approximately 40 per cent of the total allocations each year were to go to this objective, including some of the youth unemployment allocations).
- Funding employment creation initiatives in other depressed regions in the Community.
- Encouraging the implementation of innovatory projects.

Overall, the emphasis was now placed on making a contribution to the fight against structural unemployment, and easing the acute disadvantage of some special groups. Money was usually allocated to four types of initiatives: vocational training and guidance; recruitment and wage grants; resettlement and socio-vocational integration programmes in connection with geographical mobility; and services and technical advice concerning job creation. Both public and private organisations were able to apply for a Social Fund grant but the rules of the Fund required that no schemes could be financed wholly by money from Europe. For initiatives run by public bodies the Fund would grant up to 50 per cent of the costs, while for schemes run by private organisations the Fund's grant would not be more than that from a national authority. The Fund increased substantially: from about 170 million ECU in 1973 to 2,188,350 million ECU in 1985. But this should be placed in context — the Social Fund represented only about 6 per cent of the Community's total budget during that time (the Common Agricultural Policy in contrast consumed approximately 72.5 per cent).

The Operation of the European Social Fund

A long-standing criticism of the Fund was that it was organised and operated in a bureaucratic way. A study of the Fund concluded that 'it was a complex of managerial, administrative and financial issues which together have created a system cumbersome to operate, slow to decide and pay out and which operational bodies find hard to understand' (Collins 1982 p 67). The main target for much of the criticism was the Fund's budgetary arrangements: total 'appropriations' of the Fund each year were dependent on the outcome of the annual negotiations for the entire Community budget. As the Community budget was the scene of acrimonious and prolonged disputes in the late 1970s and early 1980s, the exact amount allocated to the European Social Fund was frequently not known until well into the financial year.

Obviously, this situation created considerable uncertainty. In addition, the administrators of the Fund in Brussels were restricted in the possible improvements they could make. For example, one suggestion was to make the Fund subject to long-term planning, but this was virtually impossible in the circumstances. The administrators had no way of knowing the scale and nature of the Fund's budget from one year to the next. The situation also caused difficulties for the national organisations that made applications. In particular, they experienced long delays before being told whether or not their application had been successful and, if so, the amounts they would receive. In the majority of cases, the national organisations had either to abandon the proposed project or to start it without knowing whether they would actually obtain a Social Fund grant.

Other problems made the situation even more complicated. The financial year of the Fund ran from January to December, while the financial year for most British organisations, for instance, was April to March, thus creating numerous administrative and financial difficulties. Furthermore, as the Fund's regulations laid down that grants were allocated on an annual basis only, an organisation which wanted a grant to help fund a three-year scheme, had to make three separate applications — hardly an administrative convenience. (The only exception to this rule was the innovatory projects category, for which grants for up to three years could be secured from a single application.) In other words, organisations wanting money from Europe had to carry a considerable administrative burden.

What made matters worse was that the procedure for actually allocating grants was less than straightforward. Theoretically, once a scheme was approved an initial contribution of 50 per cent of the total grant was made immediately, with the remainder of the money being given at the end of the scheme. In practice this procedure was rarely followed: many recipients of Social Fund grants complained that they had to wait two years or more before being paid any money from Brussels. In the meantime they had to meet all the expenses of the projects themselves.

Clearly these budgetary and financial arrangements made the Fund excessively cumbersome during the 1970s and early

1980s. Some of the complexities, like the mismatch between the Community's and the British financial years, could perhaps have been smoothed out by specific internal changes. But it is hard to see how the more fundamental difficulties could have been resolved without root and branch revisions of the entire Community budgetary framework at the time.

While these numerous burdens were very real, it would be misleading to attach disproportionate importance to them, since every year the Fund was flooded with applications. In fact, the Commission had to take away a certain amount of money from all successful applications. Thus, although the complexities of the system frustrated and inconvenienced national organisations, the evidence suggests they were not deterred from applying to the Fund.

The Administration of the European Social Fund

The Social Fund was also heavily criticised for its administration of the applications procedure. The justification for such complaints, however, does not appear entirely convincing. Indeed, as the Division in the Commission which administered the Fund employed only 20 staff who processed 6,000 applications annually, it could be argued that the administration was efficient.

It is valuable, in considering the administrative criticisms, to outline the procedure that existed for distributing Social Fund grants. The European Social Fund was administered in Brussels by a division of the Directorate of Social Affairs, Employment and Education (DGV). The exact allocation of grants was worked out by the staff in the Division. The eligibility criteria and other guidelines, by which staff assessed applications, were drawn up by the Social Fund Advisory Committee. This Committee comprised representatives from member states governments, the European employers' organisation, Union of Industrial and Employers' Confederations of Europe (UNICE), and the corresponding trade union body, European Trade Union Confederation (ETUC). The Committee also ratified the final allocations of grants made by Commission staff.

Within each member state a government department was given the task of coordinating the operation of the Fund within its territory and of performing a preliminary gatekeeping function. In Britain this task was assigned to the Department of Employment. Organisations within each member state received and returned their applications for Social Fund grants to their respective national departments, which assessed whether these conformed to the rules and regulations governing the Fund. Only 'eligible' applications were sent to Brussels for consideration.

The government departments did not make judgements about the merits of any application; that role was performed by the Commission. However the national departments did operate in a highly partisan fashion: each national government department aimed to send forward as many applications as possible. They gave in-depth guidance to organisations on how to make a valid application. Some promoted the existence of the Fund and encouraged individual organisations to apply to it, while others operated early deadline dates so that they would have the time to examine applications and send them back for redrafting if necessary before they were sent to Brussels.

No doubt countless other ways were used by each government department to improve the quantity and quality of applications from its country. However, the British Department of Employment was considered by Commission officials to be the most efficient national body of all the member states at promoting and processing Social Fund applications.

Great Britain and the European Social Fund

To give a better idea of how the Social Fund affected member states' employment environment, this section examines the Fund's grant allocations to Great Britain in the years between the late 1970s and the mid-1980s. Between 1981–85 Great Britain was, after Italy, the biggest recipient of Social Fund money. In 1984 this amounted to 243.7m ECU. It has been suggested that this situation arose as the result of the Commission's attempts to meet British objections to the size of its contribution to the Community budget. While this cannot be totally ruled out, an equally plausible reason was put forward by Commission officials in interviews with the author, namely, that the British applications for Social Fund grants were superior to those from other member states. In all probability it was a mixture of the two factors which secured a high proportion of Social Fund money for Britain.

Table 5 outlines the amount of money Great Britain received from the Fund from 1979 to 1984, and compares it to the level of money given to the national training agency in Britain, the Manpower Services Commission, during the same period.

Table 5 **Social Fund grants received by Great Britain compared to monies received by the Manpower Services Commission 1979–1984**

Year	Social Fund allocation to Britain (m)	MSC expenditure (m)
1979	n/a	671.2
1980	439.5	869.3
1981	136.7	1111.4
1982	257.2	1337.4
1983	323.5	1767.8
1984	250.3	2110.2

The table shows that, compared to the amounts spent on training and employment initiatives by the MSC, the Social Fund grants to Britain were miniscule. Thus, the Fund's contribution to training and employment in Britain was marginal in this period. Its role was effectively constrained by lack of resources. This explains the conclusion drawn by one commentator that 'the Social Fund would need to be expanded to a very considerable extent before it could become capable of making any real impact' (Taylor 1983 p 201).

It can be seen from the table that Social Fund allocations went to standard MSC programmes. Because these grants were paid directly into the relevant MSC budgets, it must be concluded that Social Fund money was used as a fiscal transfer

Table 6 **European Social Fund allocations to the Manpower Services Commission 1980–1986 (m)**

	1980	1981	1982	1983	1984[1]	1985	1986
Young People	57.8	67.0	121.0	n/a	137.0	90.00	107.0
Disabled Persons	8.0	12.6	17.0	n/a	7.0	11.5	1.0
Others[2]	110.9	100.9	194.8	n/a	93.4	59.0	35.0

Source: Manpower Services Commission Statistical Department
Notes

[1] It should be noted that for the years 1984 to 1985 the actual amounts allocated were not necessarily the amounts claimed. When applications were made to the Fund they were based on estimates up to a year in advance and the final claims sometimes fell short of the estimates.

[2] 'Others' classification refers to projects for women, migrants (particularly language training), regions, and technical consultancy fees. Expenditures on these individual programmes could not be obtained.

for nationally-determined labour-market policies. This further reduced the role of the Fund in Britain, since grants awarded should theoretically have gone towards complementing national employment initiatives by sponsoring innovatory and original schemes.

Perhaps the main reason why most of the grants were directed towards the centre was that the government, or more precisely a government quango (the MSC), had gradually taken over responsibility for vocational education and training during the 1980s. This trend had its origins in the 'New Training Initiative' White Paper in 1981. Paul Ryan (1984, p 27) suggests that it 'effectively buried the long-standing principle that the finance of industrial training is the responsibility of employers'. Thus, as the governmental role in training and employment increased, the possibility of using the Social Fund to develop an autonomous European dimension reduced, since all Community money simply helped pay nationally-determined labour-market policies.

The Local Authority Dimension

The only independent, non-government, impact the Social Fund had in Britain was sponsoring local authority initiatives. From about 1981 local authorities became increasingly active in trying to obtain Social Fund grants. Undoubtedly, it was the squeeze on public expenditure that prompted the turn towards Europe. But the expansion in economic development that the local authorities have experienced since the early 1980s was also important. Local authorities started initiating employment and training projects which the Social Fund aimed to support; as a result, it was only a matter of time before the two graduated towards each other.

The demand for Social Fund money from British local authorities during the early to mid 1980s far outweighed the amount on offer. As part of its approach to dealing with this problem the Commission compiled a list of priority areas based on data from labour force surveys. There were 36 priority areas (detailed in Appendix 2). Not surprisingly all these authorities received some Social Fund monies each year, but the statistics show that some 24 other 'non-priority' local authorities also benefited from Social Fund grants at some point during the five-year period.

Allocation of Social Fund money

In order to analyse the non-government dimension of the Fund in greater depth, it is necessary to identify in detail the allocation of Social Fund money on a local authority basis. This information, for the years 1981 to 1985, is presented for the first time in Appendix 2. As would be expected, most of the Social Fund grants went towards training schemes in depressed regions. However, there appeared to be a bias towards those local authorities in the priority areas which were perceived in the national context to be in most need of urgent action. For example, when Merseyside hit the headlines after the 1981 riots, the Social Fund money to the area increased substantially. The same happened when the marked deindustrialisation of the West Midlands was given widespread national publicity in 1983.

The distribution of Social Fund grants among the priority areas appeared to be skewed, with the most depressed regions obtaining much higher contributions than those deemed to be suffering from lesser social disadvantage. The extent of Social Fund contribution to local authorities was, therefore, uneven.

For example, the grants received by Greater Manchester, totalling £8.5m in 1985, must have added considerably to the scale and number of initiatives in the area, whereas the £320,000 obtained by Gwent would have helped only a few schemes. A possible by-product was that the EC may have had a higher status in the depressed regions of Great Britain.

The only discernible trend among the non-priority local authorities which received Social Fund money was that the majority were in rural areas. Some of these authorities were awarded large sums: Avon County Council received over 11m ECU for training schemes in 1985. This trend was probably due to the strong support for rural development in the Commission. It was perhaps the biggest single 'European' influence on the distribution of the Social Fund in Great Britain. However, there was less than unanimous support for this type of assistance. One commentator suggested that the opportunity cost of targeting money on rural areas was that the more needy industrial locations were starved of resources (Johnson 1986).

Effects of the Social Fund

It would be misleading to overstress the impact of the Social Fund on British local authorities in the early 1980s. Judging by the interviews conducted by the author with seven local authorities across the country, many of the projects funded by European money would have been undertaken even without funding. But, in general, within the local context the Fund did add value to employment and training initiatives. The fact that many local authorities appointed EC Liaison Officers, or made other organisational changes to maximise benefits from Europe, reinforces this conclusion. These changes were complemented by the work of the national local authorities federations which started paying greater attention to European deliberations.

Another less tangible result was that the prospect of Social Fund money induced more innovatory and experimental thinking among local authorities. Because the Fund was hugely oversubscribed, conventional training initiatives were unlikely to be awarded money. This led local authorities to open discussions with voluntary organisations, educational institutions and private businesses about the types of local training needs that existed and the best ways they could be met. The result was a greater diversity in local training. It also helped extend the thinking about training in Britain and widened the type of instruments on offer. A good case in point was training for women. At the outset there was considerable hesitancy on the part of the MSC to fund 'women only' training programmes. However, such schemes were established largely as a result of them receiving EC Social Fund grants. It soon became evident that these schemes were popular and worthwhile. Only then did they receive official (MSC) endorsement.

This was the role the Fund could have most usefully played in relation to employment and training in Britain. By encouraging and sponsoring new forms of training it could have increased the repertoire of local initiatives on offer. Another way the Fund could have extended its role was by being a 'transmission mechanism' to transfer original schemes between member states. Through this selective and complementary approach the Social Fund could have reached its maximum feasible potential. But the overall conclusion must be that the Social Fund played only a small role with regard to training and employment policies in Britain during the late 1970s and early 1980s.

The European Social Fund and the 1992 Project

Although a body of opinion regards the 1992 project as essentially a liberalisation exercise to obtain greater market integration between the member states, the Commission has always taken a wider systemic approach to the issue. In particular, the Commission sees the completion of the Internal Market Programme as much a political and social project as an economic and commercial programme. The political aspect of the 1992 programme centres on obtaining social and economic cohesion to resolve the growing regional disparities within the Community.

As a result of enlargements during the 1980s (Greece 1981

and Spain and Portugal 1985), and the widespread industrial restructuring, particularly in the heavy industries, regional problems have substantially increased within the Community. Such problems are now greater among the member states than at any time in the Community's history. To ensure that the market completion aspects of the 1992 programme would not cement or even accentuate the regional disparities, the Commission has developed a range of policies, under the rubric of economic and social cohesion, which specifically address the issue of regional divergence. Essentially these policies amount to integrating the various Community's independent funds and targeting them on a narrower set of defined problems. The reorganisation effectively brings to end one operation of the European Social Fund as an individual, stand-alone arrangement. But before addressing that issue directly it may be worthwhile outlining the Community's new approach to economic and social cohesion.

The new objectives

In its programmatic document, 'The Single Act: A New Frontier for Europe', the Commission argued that the Community's structural funds — the European Social Fund, the guidance section of the European Agricultural Guidance and Guarantee Fund (FEOGA) and the European Regional Fund (ERDF) — which had operated more or less independently from each other should be integrated, and called the European Structural Fund, in order to concentrate on a few specific objectives rather than on a number of heterogeneous ones, as had traditionally been the case. The Commission listed five primary objectives for the new integrated fund to pursue:

(1) developing 'less developed' regions ('Objective No 1');
(2) converting regions and small areas 'seriously affected by industrial decline' ('Objective No 2');
(3) combatting long-term unemployment ('Objective No 3');
(4) combatting youth unemployment ('Objective No 4')
(5) developing 'agricultural structures' and rural areas ('Objective No 5(a) and 5(b)').

The European Council agreed to the objectives and established defining criteria for 'Objective No 1' and 'Objective No 2' areas. As regards 'Objective No 1' areas, the qualifying regions were those with GDP per capita less than 75 per cent of the Community figure averaged over the past three years. In geographical terms, this definition embraces Greece, much of Spain, Portugal, Southern Italy, Ireland, Northern Ireland and the French Overseas Department. The Council also agreed that 75 per cent of ERDF was to be devoted to 'Objective No 1' areas, which would lead to the doubling of the receipts in these areas by 1992. Regions to be incorporated into 'Objective No 2' areas were those such as North-east England, Picardie in France, and Freiburg in West Germany, which are now unemployment blackspots due to the economic recession.

Underscoring these organisational changes, the member states committed themselves to doubling the Structural Fund budget from 7,400m ECU in the 1988 draft budget to a total of 13,000m ECU in 1992. If adhered to, this commitment will represent a major change in the direction of Community spending. In particular, it will mean that the proportion of the overall Community budget allocated to the Structural Funds will have risen from 18 per cent in 1986 to well over 30 per cent by 1992.

A number of qualitative administrative and financial changes have also been introduced into the operation of the Funds. Among the most important changes is the shift from a project approach to a programme approach. Previously, the standard practice of the Funds was to assist in the financing of nationally-defined projects on an *ad hoc* and uncoordinated basis. Moreover, little to no monitoring occurred to assess the extent to which the funded projects achieved their objectives. As one politician noted in relation to the ERDF, 'the Regional Fund operated on a red cross basis, with handouts here and there. There was no plan for regional policy at all in the Community; it was a series of Funds' (John Hume 1988, p 108).

The Programme Approach

To reduce these shortcomings, the Council agreed to a new programme approach which involves five changes to the existing system. In the future, initiatives are to be largely programmes involving a range of activities, which may have a considerable impact on the local economy over a period of years. So, instead of using the various Funds to help finance a road infrastructure project, for example, or an individual training scheme, as was traditionally the case, the new programme approach will sponsor only those initiatives which incorporate both types of scheme. Previously, as seen with the Social Fund, all the Funds more or less operated as external financial benefactors to national projects, but had little or no say in the creation, design or running of such schemes. Under the new approach this passive role will end, for the Commission intends to build partnerships between Community institutions and local public authorities so that it can have a greater say in defining and shaping programmes from the very outset.

The Commission also intends to step up the monitoring and assessment of funded programmes to ensure that targets are being met and to enable it to draw lessons from the successes and the failures so to help policy development in the future. A final revision to the existing approach will be the reorganisation of other Community institutions, for example the European Investment Bank, so that more of their activities can be directed towards assisting the drive for economic and social cohesion.

Although many of the specific operational parts of the new programme approach still need to be worked out, it shows that the Commission is determined to tackle the question of regional and social imbalances within the Community.

The likely effect of reform is that the lion's share of the Structural Fund relating to employment and training schemes will go to regionally disadvantaged parts of the Community. If this is the case then, despite the near doubling of the Structural Fund, the richer Northern European countries, including Britain, will in all probability experience a decline in cash from Europe for employment and training schemes.

Not surprisingly, the British government is holding out against Community money on employment schemes having a regional bias. The Conservative administration argues that the Structural Fund should not be constrained by geographical limits; worth-while training schemes in inner cities should have as much chance of obtaining grants as similar initiatives in the depressed parts of the Community. But because the British case will be seen as being motivated by self-interest, it is unlikely that the other member states will be persuaded by it. In all probability a large part of the Community money for labour market schemes will be linked to the theme of regional development.

In addition to experiencing a decline in the number of grants for training, etc, the Commission's new programme approach may also have a telling impact on Britain. Hitherto, as explained earlier, the Social Fund in Britain has been used mostly to give financial support to nationally-defined training programmes with relatively little money going to local projects. But this situation may have to change to make way for the new emphasis on multifaceted area or regional programmes. In the future, grants from the new Structural Fund may be concentrated in certain regions, or sub-regions such as Teesside or Clydeside, while national (Training Agency) schemes and other projects from different parts of the country lose out.

Chapter 4
European Community Social Legislation

The European Community is distinctive among international institutions in that it is invested with more authority to intervene directly in the economic and political affairs of the member states. So, as regards to employment and industrial relations matters, the most direct way the EC may influence member states is through developing a body of Community-wide labour legislation. It was not until the early 1970s, however, that the idea of the Community legislating in the employment and labour fields, beyond issues relating to the free movement of workers, gained currency. The desire to have a wider range of labour statutes was largely the result of a new-found commitment among the member states at the time to develop a more positive and interventionist Community social policy. Politically, this commitment was made explicit at the Paris Summit of 1972. There, the member states declared that developing a strong social dimension to the Community was as important as establishing economic and monetary union (Shanks 1977).

The Development of EC Social Legislation in the 1970s

In 1974 the Commission launched the Social Action Programme which set out three broad principles to guide future Community action in the social sphere

- full and better employment
- the improvement of living and working conditions
- greater participation of workers in the economic and social decisions of the Community (Commission of the EC 1974).

After the Council ratified the programme, the Commission began devising concrete social policies relating to the different policy areas. One group of policies had the objective of using the Community's legal machinery to establish a set of statutes relating to employment rights and conditions. A detailed description of each piece of EC social policy is not required here, as a full description of each individual initiative is given elsewhere (Teague 1988). But it may be useful to give a brief summary of the initiatives under various categories.

Workers rights

Action here has included the ratification by the Council of a series of Directives aimed at protecting the rights of workers in cases of mass dismissals, transfer of undertakings and insolvencies.

Health and safety

The Commission has made ten proposals for Directives on the protection of workers exposed to physical and chemical agents at work, and one on the prevention of major accident hazards due to chemical agents. So far seven have been adopted by the Council.

Company organisation and participation

Altogether, the Commission has produced 12 draft Directives and several resolutions relating to company organisation. The objective of these proposals has been to obtain a degree of harmonisation in company law across the Community. Because of technical and legal reasons, some of the Directives have not yet been ratified. The only one which is relevant to the analysis here is the draft Fifth Directive which aims to establish formal participation structures in companies within the Community. This has been at the drafting stage for about 15 years and there are still no signs of it being ratified by the Council. Another proposed Directive — the so called 'Vredeling Directive' — which aims to introduce formal employee information and consultation procedures into certain companies within the Community, has met with universal opposition from employers and, for this reason, also remains on the drafting table.

Equal opportunities

This is the area where Community action has been most extensive. The 1975 Equal Pay Directive obliged member states to abolish all discrimination between the pay of men and women arising from their laws, regulations and administrative provisions. This statute was reinforced by the Equal Treatment Directive of the following year. In 1978 the Community extended its powers against sex discrimination into the field of statutory social security through the Social Security Directive. Another Directive applying similar principles to occupational social security schemes was adopted in 1986. In addition, a number of rulings made by the Court of Justice have had far-reaching implications for women in all member states.

Working time arrangements

At the end of the 1970s, the Commission started to place greater emphasis on developing labour market policies. A number of initiatives were produced: a Recommendation on the reorganisation and reduction of working time; a draft Directive on safeguarding the rights of part-time and temporary workers; a draft Recommendation encouraging firms to introduce flexible retirement schemes; and finally, a draft Directive creating statutory provision on Parental Leave and Leave for Family Reasons. Apart from a modified version of the flexible retirement Recommendation, none of these proposals has been passed by the Council.

The Nature of EC Social Legislation

The social legislation adopted by the Council falls into three categories as regards its effects on member states labour law.

One category is the legislation which, when introduced, was designed to match, or to bring about minor changes to, the corresponding laws already in place within the member states. Typical of this form of legislation, generally viewed as benign, are the Mass Dismissals and Insolvency Directives as well as most of the health and safety Directives.

Another category, consisting mainly of a small number of

health and safety Directives, can be seen as having a far-reaching impact on prevailing national law and commercial practices in certain confined areas. Thus, the various Directives relating to the protection of workers handling dangerous chemical substances obliged many companies in the chemical and textiles industries substantially to change their health and safety practices while, at the same time, enterprises in other economic sectors remained unaffected. As these Directives were largely based on the findings of scientific research, and as they affected the safety of people at work, the member states have in the main complied fully with them.

The Transfer of Undertakings Directive and the group of equal opportunities Directives constitute a third category, which has been the most important and substantive source of EC social legislation. Several case studies show that when adopted these statutes went beyond corresponding legislation in the member states (Landau 1985 and Hoskyns 1987).

Thus, by passing the Directives, the member states established a body of labour law at Community level which could potentially have had a far-reaching impact on individual national employment environments.

However, evidence suggests that member states are using their control over the legal ports of entry, through which Community Directives are passed into national law, to limit the impact of these pieces of EC social legislation. Several examples from the British context support this assessment. On a number of occasions, Britain has been found guilty by the Court of Justice of not fully implementing Community equality legislation. The British Government introduced legislation to comply with these rulings, but some argue that these amendments still fail to bring British law into line with Community law (Rubenstein 1984).

Another example is the Transfer of Undertakings Directive. Hepple (1982) argues that this Directive was introduced into Britain in an underhand way. In particular, for the first time in the field of labour law, a Community Directive was passed into British law by means of a Regulation rather than by an Act of Parliament. With minor exceptions, Regulations, unlike Acts of Parliament, do not make actual amendments to existing legislation. As a result, the Regulations introducing the Transfer of Undertakings Directive sit uneasily with existing national law, creating considerable confusion in the courts — a situation roundly condemned by the Advisory, Conciliation and Arbitration Service (ACAS) in its 1987 report. Hepple goes on to argue that the clauses of the Regulation 'are not in full compliance with the spirit or intent of the Directive' (Hepple 1982, p 28).

Although perhaps the worst offender, Britain is not the only one failing to implement in full EC social legislation. Indeed, on Community equality law, the Commission has found it necessary to take infringement proceedings against all member states (except Greece) because their legislation did not meet the requirements of the Community procedures (McCrudden 1987).

Social Legislation and the Role of Direct Applicability

Theoretically, where the contents of a Directive have not been properly or fully passed into national law, individuals can invoke the Community law in national courts as long as it is *directly applicable*. Direct applicability is the legal term used to describe those aspects of Community legislation which confer rights (and obligations) on individuals that are superior to national legislation.

However, there are strict limits to the extent to which the direct applicability principle covers Directives (Wyatt 1984). In the first place, the consensus view is that if a Directive is unconditional and sufficiently precise and has not been properly implemented by a member state then individuals can invoke it in national courts. But because many Directives are open-ended and indefinite, and because it is legally difficult to prove whether or not member states have fully and properly implemented a Directive, there are only a few areas where it can be regarded as having direct applicability. Furthermore, as a result of several Court of Justice rulings, it has been established that the direct applicability of a Directive is confined to the public sector: it cannot be used to impose obligations on companies. Thus, for example, the Transfer of Undertakings Directive is not directly applicable as it only relates to the commercial (private) sector and not to the public sector.

In the situation where a Community Directive has not been properly implemented into national law and where it is not directly applicable, citizens of the respective member states may not be able to enjoy the possible benefits of the EC law. The only way this situation can be rectified is if the Commission launches 'non-compliance' or infringement proceedings against the national government at the Court of Justice. But such a legal recourse is not entirely satisfactory (Docksey 1988). Because a large number of cases are waiting to be heard at any one time, a 'non-compliance' case may take two years before it is dealt with by the Court.

Equality legislation

In the area of equality legislation, there is more scope for individuals and groups to use the Community's legal machinery to challenge national laws and practices. Article 119 of the Treaty of Rome lays down that member states should pursue the policy of equal pay for equal work. The legal significance of this Article is that it is part of the primary legislation of the Community, and is therefore directly applicable in the public and private sectors. Equal opportunities interest groups have used Article 119 to bring cases before national courts and obtain rulings which extend women's rights in the Community.

The process works along the following lines. The case is first brought before the national court: in Great Britain this would be an industrial tribunal. Because it is European law that is being used, and if the issue is contentious, the national court will almost certainly transfer the case to the European Court of Justice for a ruling. When the European Court of Justice adopts its decision it is passed back to the national court, which then implements it into domestic legislation.

The first case was brought before the Court in 1976. Invoking Article 119, Madame Defrenne, who worked for Belgium's Sabena Airlines, successfully claimed equal pay with a male cabin steward. Numerous other cases invoking the Article have also reached the Court and the subsequent rulings have had wide beneficial implications for women throughout the Community.

A few British cases can also serve as examples. Wendy Smith, a manageress in a pharmaceutical company, won her case on the grounds that, although she took up her post four months after her predecessor, a man, had left, a woman can legitimately compare her pay with that of a man previously doing the same job. Two women employees of Lloyds Bank succeeded in their claim that the Bank's occupational pension scheme discriminated in favour of male workers, both as regards to contributions and with respect to certain other benefits. Mrs Jenkins, a part-time worker, established that in certain circumstances part-time workers should not be paid less *pro rata* than full-time employees. As a result of these and other cases, the Court of Justice has played an important role in upholding and extending the Community's equality law at a time when few new pieces of legislation in the area were being passed by the Council.

Despite these well-publicised Court of Justice rulings in equality cases, the consensus among legal opinion is that the extent to which Community equal opportunity legislation can effect national employment environments depends on the operational interpretation given to these laws by national courts (Rubenstein 1987 and Treu 1986). If a national court adopts a narrow interpretation of the statutes transferring an EC Directive into domestic law, then it will have only a limited impact. Conversely, if a broad definition is taken then the impact will evidently be more wideranging. Hepple (1987) suggests that, as a rule, national courts will tend to be cautious in their interpretation of EC-inspired legislation. But it is too early to draw such a conclusion for in several member states there are still many test cases to be heard which will set the exact legal parameters of national laws based on Community legislation. In fact, recent judgements in some of the test cases in Britain (eg, the House of Lords' rulings in the Hayward and Pickstone cases) contradict Hepple's conclusions, as they have widened the operational scope of EC-induced national equality legislation.

Overall, however, the conclusion must be that while the Community has adopted a body of quasi-supranational labour law which has had some impact on the employment environment in each member state, the extent of its influence should, on paper at least, have been much greater. The use of the legal ports of entry by some member states, the limitations of Directives as a Community legal instrument, the deficiencies of the Commission's non-compliance procedures and the complexities and uncertainties surrounding some aspects of EC legislation, have all interacted to soften the influence of EC labour law on member states. With the changes introduced by the Single European Act to resolve the backlog of cases in the European Court of Justice, and with many test cases soon to be heard by national courts, some of the obstacles preventing the Community having a greater bearing on labour affairs in the member states may be removed. But such an outcome cannot be predicted with any certainty.

Why have so many proposals failed to get ratified?

An equally important question to consider is why so many of the Commission's social policy proposals have not been ratified by the Council. Two main factors are at work: the limits to the harmonisation approach adopted by the Commission in the 1970s and the clash between the British Government and the Commission on labour market reform in the 1980s.

The limits to labour market harmonisation

During the 1970s the key social policy proposals of the Commission — most notably the draft Fifth Directive on company law and the popularly known draft Vredeling Directive — were heavily influenced by integrationist principles (Pipkorn 1984 and Docksey 1985). In particular, the Commission wanted to bring about a measure of harmonisation in the member states' industrial relations systems so that the internal market could work more effectively. In practice, this involved the Commission scanning the member states for the 'best practices' on particular employment-related issues and then making these the basis of a draft Directive. But the Commission considerably underestimated the problems associated with trying to harmonise employment policies and practices across the member states.

A basic tenet of comparative labour law is that transferring industrial relations practices across national frontiers is fraught with difficulties. As one labour lawyer put it,

> We cannot take for granted that rules or institutions are transplantable . . . any attempt to use a pattern of law outside the environment of its origin continues to entail the risk of rejection. Labour law is part of a system, and the consequences of change in one aspect of the system depends upon the relationship between all elements of the system. Since these relationships may not be similar between the two societies, the effects of similar legislation may differ significantly as between the two settings. (Blanpain 1985, p 7)

The results of the clash between the integrationist objectives of the Commission and the apparent limitations to transferring employment policies and practices across frontiers are well known. The Fifth Directive was first proposed in 1972, and despite endless rounds of negotiations has yet to be adopted. The proposed Vredeling Directive sparked off a major controversy involving employers, unions and governments at the national, European and international levels. As a result, it too failed to be ratified by the Council. From this evidence Blanpain suggests,

> The conclusion is clear: rules relating to the power relations in the industrial relations systems and also in society as a whole will be the most difficult to transplant. . . . This is why the proposed Directive providing for more workers' participation in the ten EEC member countries, the so called Fifth Directive, is not on the books: it affects the power relationship in enterprises. (Blanpain 1985, p 10)

Thus, there appears to be strict limits to the strategy of 'harmonising' employment practices across the Community. Past experience shows that proposed Directives in this mould have been over-ambitious and have ended in embarrassing failures.

The arguments about the limits of harmonisation are also evoked to explain why the set of proposals on working time (ie the draft Part-Time Workers, Temporary Workers and Parental Leave Directives and the Recommendation on the reorganisation of working time) produced in the early 1980s failed to get adopted by the Council. But the applicability of this explanation here is questionable simply because the degree of harmonisation which these initiatives would have entailed was not in fact very extensive. For instance, the draft Recommendation on the reorganisation and reduction of working time had no legally binding force and thus did not commit the member states to any specific action. Furthermore, as Great Britain was the only country with no legal provisions on the subject, and as the specific clauses were widely regarded as not being far-reaching, the proposed Parental Leave Directive cannot be seen as an attempt at excessive or monolithic harmonisation. Although the Part-Time Workers draft Directive would have entailed significant legal changes in certain member states, particularly Britain, some considered there to be enough manoeuvrability for a compromise to be negotiated (House of Lords 1982). Even a British employers' organisation accepted that while all the proposals would have an impact in their respective fields they would not have any fundamental bearing on the British employment environment or that of other member states (EEF 1984). Thus, there would appear to be insufficient grounds for rejecting the working time initiatives on the basis that they would lead to uniform harmonisation.

Social protection *v* labour market deregulation

The second factor, a clash between the social protectionist aims of the Commission and the deregulation outlook of the British Government, provides a more convincing explanation of why these latter proposals were not ratified by the Council of Ministers. Commission officials have openly made it plain that the motive behind its proposals on working time arrangements was to afford workers in the Community a degree of social protection rather than to obtain a level of harmonisation in these policy areas (Morley 1982). However, the

Conservative Government along with British employers' organisations strongly opposed the initiatives, arguing that they would constrain operational flexibility by imposing restrictions on companies' relations with employers. Their opposition has led the Conservative Government to adopt an uncompromising stance on these proposals inside Council, and even to using its veto on occasions.

The extent of the British Government's opposition is indicated by the fate of the proposed Recommendation on the Reduction of Working Time. The recommendation, which had no legally binding force, was strongly opposed by Norman Tebbit, the then Secretary of State for Employment, inside the Council on the basis that it would pave the way for bureaucratic interference in British labour market procedures. In an effort to accommodate the viewpoint of the British Government, amendments were made to the text which emphasised that any reduction in working time must be linked to corresponding cuts in unit labour costs, either directly or through productivity gains. However, such changes were obviously insufficient for the British Government since it blocked these revised proposals when they came before the Council (Welsh 1987).

At the heart of the clash between the Conservative Government and the Commission over EC social policy were two opposing views about how the labour market should be reformed to deal with unemployment within the Community. For the British Government, the job creation process would begin again only if the labour market was freed from the rigidities — most notably government legal regulation — that had developed since the Second World War. Thus, it wanted the Community to adopt the same type of deregulatory measures as it had introduced in Britain (Lee 1987). The Commission did not share the deregulatory approach of the British Government. While accepting the need for greater flexibility in the labour market, the Commission did not think this needed the abolition or streamlining of the legal rights of workers. It preferred a strategy which 'meshed' flexibility initiatives with social protectionist measures (CEC 1987b). As mentioned earlier, these contrasting views about the direction of EC social policy, and in particular its legislative dimension, resulted in a complete impasse on the subject in the early 1980s.

The stalemate continued from the turn of the 1980s until 1985 with the result that virtually no action was taking place on social legislation. Then a new Commission came to office under the Presidency of Jacques Delors. It was determined to restart the mechanism of European integration, which included resolving the deadlock on social policy matters. Thus, not long after taking office, the Delors administration launched a major new initiative on social affairs. At the same time, the Conservative Government began to realise that it could not go on simply rejecting Commission initiatives without making some alternative proposals. As a result, on the wake of the Delors initiative, the Conservative Government launched its own plan for the future direction of Community social policy. Both initiatives are examined more fully below.

L'Espace Sociale initiative

When Jacques Delors became President of the Commission in 1985 one of his main objectives was to resolve the stalemate on whether or not there should be a legal dimension to Community social policy. But he faced a dilemma: if the Commission continued trying to establish a social dimension to the Community via the legislative route it risked being accused of forcing change against national patterns; but if no Community legislation existed, it could result in EC social policy being nothing more than a series of non-binding guidelines. As a way out of this dilemma, Delors put forward the concept of *l'espace sociale* — which literally translated means 'social space' or 'social area'. A good deal of confusion existed about the policy implications of the idea of a European social area. Some perceived it as a new policy formulation, but it was actually first put forward by the French Government in 1981. At that stage the European Parliament took the idea to mean a European employment plan.

Part of the reason why so much confusion reigned about the notion was that nobody spelt out clearly what it would mean in practice. From the evidence that exists, it appeared that Delors linked the idea of *l'espace sociale* to the central objective of the new Commission, that is the completion of the internal market by 1992. In particular, he envisaged *l'espace sociale* as establishing some sort of equivalence of social standards inside the Community so as to avoid 'social dumping' (see below) — the situation whereby high-wage economies could lose out to low-wage economies or where countries effectively export their unemployment by cutting established employees' benefits when the remaining trade barriers are removed (Beretta 1987).

However, it is far from clear how Delors intended to implement his notion. One element of his plan seems to have been the establishment, or perhaps more accurately the re-establishment, of a social dialogue between employers and trade unions, the so-called social partners, with the purpose of establishing common agreements on various employment and work-related issues. Thus, when presenting the Commission's programme for 1985 to the European Parliament, Delors said that 'policies based on agreements and negotiations between management and labour are one of the cornerstones of this new social area' (cited in European Parliament 1986, p 12). Some interpreted this proposal as yet another attempt to establish some form of European collective bargaining (Lodge 1986).

Although many in the Commission and in European trade unions still harbour that desire, the social dialogue in question seems to be limited to the formation of social policy, rather than bargaining on wages or employment conditions. In particular, the intention appeared to be to base EC legislation on agreements emerging from a social dialogue between management and labour rather than relying on the Commission for proposals. In other words, the trade unions and employers would become the initiators of policy in the social field. It was such thinking that lay behind Delors's statement to UNICE and the ETUC in 1985 that if they entered into a social dialogue the Commission would refrain from developing any new social policy initiatives.

In practice the significance of Delors's plan was that it

represented a withdrawal from the 'monolithic harmonisation' approach adopted by the Commission in the 1970s. Under this approach, the Commission not only laid down the social policy objectives of a Directive, but also the mechanism and methods by which these objectives were to be reached. By having the social partners initiate social proposals, Delors hoped that they would focus on policy principles and objectives and leave open the question of how these were to be implemented, so that member states would be free to introduce them within their existing industrial relations frameworks. In other words, Delors was seeking a convergence in the employment and labour policy goals of the member states, rather than the standardisation of industrial relations institutions and processes.

The Val Duchesse Experiment

As a first step towards creating a European social area, two working parties involving the social partners were set up, one relating to macro-economic policy and employment, and the other covering new technology and work. The precise status of these working groups, which became known as the 'Val Duchesse talks', was unclear. For the European employers' organisation, UNICE, the working parties were solely a forum in which the employers would discuss social and employment matters with the trade unions and the Commission. However, UNICE made it clear that it was unwilling to enter into any dialogue which sought to establish binding agreements (Tyszkiewiez 1986). The view of the European trade unions' ETUC was that the Val Duchesse talks were preparing the groundwork for effective (legislative) action in selected social policy areas (ETUC 1987). For its part, the Commission appeared to be of the view that any agreement arising from the talks would map out future Community action, some of which would be legislative.

Findings of the working parties

The differences about the status of the Val Duchesse talks surfaced when the two working parties came to communicate their findings. The employers insisted that the final texts should be described as joint opinions and not as joint agreements, arguing that an agreement tied the partners to certain arrangements or actions, while an opinion was an open-ended expression of a view or judgement on a particular matter.

The working party on macro-economic policy and employment produced its joint opinion first. This was largely based on the economic programme proposed by the Commission in its Annual Economic Report 1986–87. It suggested three central objectives for Community and member state economic policy: a mild form of reflation through public and infrastructural investment; moderation in wage settlements; and the control of inflation. The working party on new technology sat for much longer since it found considerable difficulty in concluding a joint opinion. Finally one was produced, but this was loosely worded, binding neither the trade unions nor employers to any specific action. (The opinions of the two Val Duchesse working parties are reproduced in Appendix 4.)

The outcome of the two working parties dealt a major blow to Delors's objective that the social partners should be the initiators of Community policy in the employment and labour affairs fields. Before the employers would sign the final texts, he had to give them an undertaking that the Commission would not propose any legislation on the basis of the joint opinions. Thus, the idea of a social dialogue between management and labour being a 'cornerstone' of *l'espace sociale* appears to be destroyed. One tangible benefit of the Val Duchesse talks, however, has been the restoration of good working relations, which were severely strained during the early 1980s, between the social partners. For this reason the talks are continuing (the social partners are now discussing flexibility and adaptability of the labour market), although their importance has diminished.

Labour Market Flexibility

As an alternative to the Delors project, the British Government produced its own plan for the future of Community social policy. In devising this plan the Thatcher administration wanted to check the intention of Delors, but it was also eager to appear in a more constructive light on social policy matters. The British Government was conscious of the fact that it was bad politics to be seen continually blocking Commission social policy initiatives.

The Action Programme

The centrepiece of the British Government proposal was to redirect Community social policy around the themes of labour market flexibility and deregulation (Department of Employment 1986). Thus, it wanted the idea of establishing further European regulatory employment legislation abandoned and the statutes already in place streamlined. Instead it wanted the Community to pursue policies which would encourage new flexible employment patterns and working conditions and help create a larger and more dynamic small business sector in Europe. However, the ingenuity of this proposal, known formally as the Action Programme for Employment Growth, lies not in its contents, which were only a version of policies being enacted in Great Britain, but in the skilful way the British Government manoeuvred it to the centre of the social policy agenda.

Realising that to present the initiative as purely British courted the danger of it being rejected by other member states, the Conservative Government set out to obtain co-sponsors for the proposal. After much behind-the-scenes lobbying, the British secured the Italian and Irish Governments as co-signatories. With their support the proposal could be safely placed on the Community's negotiation table. For the Commission to have opposed the initiative either directly or by proxy when it had been signed by three member states would have been outside protocol.

Thus without encountering any serious opposition the Action Programme was discussed by the member states at the December 1986 meeting of the European Council. The only reservation voiced on the proposal was that it made no reference to the social dialogue principle. But after minor amendments were made to the text to accommodate this criticism the proposal was ratified unanimously. On paper the Conservative Government had pulled off a remarkable victory, for it is seldom that a proposal which is not supported by the Commission is adopted by the Council.

The Commission's counter-strategy

Theoretically, the Council's resolution obliged the Commission to develop a wide range of labour market flexibility initiatives completely at odds with its traditional approach to social policy. In an effort to prevent the Commission from fudging the issue, the Council resolution stipulated that it had to make six-monthly progress reports. However, a reading of the first progress report reveals a subtle counter-strategy on the part of the Commission to ensure that the themes of decentralisation and deregulation would not dominate Community social policies (Commission of the EC 1987c).

In particular, the Commission divided the Action Programme into separate initiatives and classified them under existing Community programmes and initiatives. This implied that the British initiatives involved, at best, only a revision of current programmes and not a radical new policy direction. Therefore, the Action Programme's suggestions on labour mobility were portrayed as merely a new dimension to the long-standing policy goal of obtaining the free movement of workers inside the Community rather than part of a deregulatory programme for the European labour market. Similarly, the various measures listed in the Programme to improve the conditions and training for small and medium-sized enterprises were interpreted as extending and giving fresh impetus to an already established commitment. Moreover, the Commission in the report gave as much weight to the progress of the social dialogue at the Val Duchesse meetings as to other aspects of the Council's resolution, even though it represented a relatively small part of the text. In essence, the Commission was using its control over the policy making machinery to ensure that a programme to which it was opposed would not be implemented, or at least not fully implemented.

Certainly the Commission had not given up the idea of social protection. In its report on Social Developments in

1986 (published in April 1987, three months after the Council had ratified the Action Programme for Employment Growth) the following statement was included:

> the Commission intends in the near future to devise new proposals and initiatives aimed at achieving the goal of social cohesion at Community level. These proposals will be drawn up following consultations with the main organisations representing employees and workers and should contribute to alleviating existing imbalances within the Community through the establishment of a safety net of social protection and the strengthening of consultation at the Community level (CEC 1987d, p 16).

Even though the British Government was unhappy with the stance adopted by the Commission in the report and with the actual progress made towards individual measures, it did not register strong opposition to the contents of the progress report, but merely passed on an informal communication of its dissatisfaction. By and large, the reason for this low key response is that Kenneth Clarke, the main architect of the Action Programme, was no longer at the Department of Employment and the new incumbent team had neither the knowledge nor interest to pursue the matter seriously. Thus, the British attempt to redirect EC social policy towards a deregulatory approach appears to have lost its way. Little work is being done on the Action Programme — a second progress report is now long overdue and the Commission does not seem eager to publish one. While it would be premature to say that the British initiative is 'dead', it is certainly in need of reviving if it is going to have any discernible impact.

Social Policy and the Single European Act

The upshot of these proposals and counter-proposals is that, despite numerous initiatives and much negotiations on the subject in recent years, the future direction of Community social policy, at least in the legislative field, remains uncertain. The situation is only partially clarified by the Single European Act [SEA] adopted by the member states to give the 1992 programme a legal base (Lodge 1986). The clauses in the SEA relating to social policy are somewhat confusing. In particular, Article 100A [2] makes the 'rights and interests of employed persons' clearly a matter for decision by unanimous voting only.

However, Article 118A, which covers issues open to majority voting, lays down that 'member states shall pay particular attention to encouraging improvements in the working environment as regards the health and safety of workers'. Thus it seems certain that health and safety will be a matter for qualified majority under the SEA (see Appendix 1). And, if the Commission's health and safety action programme is anything to go by, the Community's legislative action in this area will increase substantially in forthcoming years (CEC 1987e).

The reference to the 'working environment' in the clause has triggered a debate about whether or not the Commission will be able to introduce proposals on other aspects of working conditions to be decided by qualified majority voting. While the prevailing view is that it will not be able to do so, in all likelihood the legal uncertainty will be resolved only by a test case before the European Court of Justice.

With the SEA not clearly defining the exact parameters to EC social policy, particularly in the legislative field, in the context of 1992 a golden opportunity to put an end to the infighting, involving mainly the Commission and the British Government, in this area was missed. As a result, by the end of 1987, the Commission and the British appeared locked in a war of attrition in which neither had enough authority or support to triumph, but each had sufficient capacity to check the design of the other. It seemed like the classic stalemate situation.

More recently, however, there are signs that a shift is occurring in favour of the Commission and others who want to see a social dimension to the 1992 project which increases the Community's regulation of the European labour market. It is hard to pinpoint exactly what has caused this shift, but there appears no doubt that active canvassing for a positive social programme by Jacques Delors, as a complement to the 1992 SEA, has had an important influence. Whatever the full explanation, there is now keener interest and wider support for the notion of a *dirigiste* (more regulatory) Community social policy. Particular interest is focused on the notion of a 'plinth of social rights' as the foundation to a social dimension to the 1992 project.

The Belgian Initiative

The origins of the plinth of social rights idea lie in a proposal put forward by Alan Hansenne, Belgium's Employment Minister, during that country's Presidency in the first half of 1987. Initially, the proposal was a hastily prepared response to the British Government's Action Programme for Employment Growth, but it quickly developed into a fully-fledged alternative strategy to this decentralised option for Community social policy.

When the Belgian Government took over the Presidency from the British at the start of 1987, it was concerned that the Action Programme might lead to a Community-wide drive to streamline employment protection legislation and other legal rights of workers. To prevent such policies from being implemented, the Belgium Government produced the social rights proposal. While recognising the need for greater adaptability in the European labour market, the Belgian initiative also held that any Community programme in this area should not undermine established statutory guarantees for workers (Hansenne 1987). To ensure this did not happen the Belgian Government proposed that the Community should establish a plinth of social rights.

A non-exhaustive list to form the basis of a plinth of social rights was submitted by the Belgians. It includes:

- Trade union freedom and the right of organisation and collective bargaining.
- Prior information and consultation for workers where there are technological innovations and other major innovations in an undertaking.
- The right of every worker to be covered by a collective convention or professional agreement, whatever the work régime.
- The right of part-time workers to normal social security

benefits, a freely negotiated work contract and the right to be represented in collective bargaining.

- A ban on excessive renewals of fixed term contracts.
- Access for every worker, in the framework of his working relations, to continuous training opportunities.
- The right of workers in the various forms of atypical work, to social security benefits and protection as regards working hours.
- The right of workers, whatever their working régime, to protective measures for health and safety.
- The right of workers to fair pay to enable them and their families to enjoy a decent standard of living.

The list of social rights closely resembles the provisions of the European Social Charter which is operated by the Council of Europe and is a sister to the European Convention of Human Rights, although without the same legally binding status. Therefore, it appears that the Belgians wanted the Community to adopt something similar to this Charter.

Under the title of *The Adaptability of the European Economy*, the Belgian Government submitted its proposal to the Council meeting of June 1987. Although the member states did not adopt a Resolution, a statement was made on the proposal recommending that it be sent to the social partners for further consideration as part of the Val Duchesse talks. Some member states, particularly Great Britain, saw sending the proposal there as a tidy way of sidestepping a potentially awkward issue. But instead of sinking into obscurity, the proposal has attracted considerable attention as a possible key aspect of a social dimension to the 1992 project.

The 'Social Dumping' Argument

The idea of a plinth of social rights has received much interest largely because it is seen as a possible way of offsetting 'social dumping' within a completely liberalised internal market. As the notion of social dumping is increasingly being used in discussions about 1992 it may be useful to explain what is meant by the term. Probably the most important point to note is that the term eludes a precise and clear definition, but in the context of 1992, it is being used to describe the potentially adverse and retrogressive effects of a deregulated and decentralised European labour market.

For example, one scenario depicted by the advocates of the social dumping thesis is that a liberalised internal market without a foundation of employment rights may lead peripheral member states to try to take advantage of their relatively low wage status *vis-à-vis* West Germany and other north European countries (Boyer 1988). In particular, they may attempt to restrain artificially the future growth of wages and other social charges so as either to increase exports or to reduce the penetration of their home market. By following such policies peripheral member states would in effect be exporting potential domestic unemployment to other member states.

Price competition

If the peripheral member states were to follow such a course (which, under a decentralised labour market régime, would be a logical route for them to follow), then the rational response of the richer countries would be to try to reduce their labour and social benefits. Such retaliatory moves could trigger cost- and price-reducing battles between the member states, particularly in the more traditional product sectors which are price sensitive. An extensive price war would be highly destabilising for the Community's economy: effective demand would fall as governments cut budgetary expenditure and adopt restrictive monetary policies; and the much needed drive to upgrade the quality of existing products, to develop new products and to master new production processes, would be stalled as managers and governments became more concerned with obtaining competitive advantages through cost reductions. Overall, it is feared that there would be no winners from these policies as all the member states would probably experience a fall in employment.

Possibilities of relocation

In addition to an increase in price competition between member states, the advocates of the social dumping thesis also argue that a decentralised and deregulated 'Europe without frontiers' may lead to large companies pursuing commercial strategies which further segments the Community's labour market into two distinctive spatial spheres (Lipietz 1988 and Leborgne and Lipietz 1988). Specifically, large companies may reorganise their operations so that complex and technical production tasks are located in northern Europe, where workers are more highly skilled, while the labour-intensive and low-skilled functions are sited in southern Europe where wages are low.

To some extent the social dumping argument is a reworking of a long-standing theme in the debate about EC social policy. Ever since the formation of the Common Market, one line of thought has been that social and labour standards (laws, institutions and conditions) need harmonising so that no trading distortions will occur as a result of some member states having more advanced provisions than others (Vandamme 1984). As outlined earlier, this line of thought underpinned the Commission's first active social policy initiatives. But in real terms this viewpoint enjoyed only minority support during the 1970s and early 1980s. At that time the dominant outlook was that the degree of divergence between the social standards of member states was not so significant as to have an adverse effect on trade relations or patterns (Wallace and Hodges 1981). This argument continues to be influential, but not, it appears, to its former extent, largely because the social dumping argument has gained support.

The social dumping thesis is currently enjoying greater favour for two reasons:

- The entry of Spain, Portugal and Greece has made the divergence in social standards widen appreciably, thus increasing the possibility of trade distortions and price wars.
- The globalisation of business strategy has significantly increased the likelihood that large firms will think in core/periphery terms within a liberalised European internal market.

By creating a Community-wide basis of statutory employment conditions, it is suggested that a plinth of social rights would establish norms and conventions in the European labour market mediating against deregulatory or cost reducing behaviour. An added attraction of the plinth of social rights idea is that instead of leading to the monolithic or uniform harmonisation of employment policies and practices across the member states, it would establish provisions which could be introduced within the framework of existing national industrial relations systems.

Towards a European Social Constitution

If a concrete proposal for a plinth of social rights were to come before the European Council in the next year or so, the British Conservative administration would unquestionably use its veto to block its passage. With this spectre on the horizon, attention has been focused on the exact legal status of a plinth of social rights and how it should be introduced. For instance, should these rights be directly applicable, like some of the equal opportunities legal provisions? Or should they be more in the mould of the worker protection Directives and merely parallel national laws?

One leading expert on European employment and labour law has suggested that the Treaty of Rome may allow EC institutions to be given the legal powers to review national law and practice against the yardstick of fundamental social rights. It is worth quoting him at length on the subject.

> Since under Article 5 of the Treaty, member states must take all 'appropriate measures' to fulfil their Treaty obligations, and these are said by the Court of Justice to include those fundamental social rights which are enshrined in the European Social Charter and the European Convention of Human Rights, there seems to be no reason why member states should not be compelled to observe such rights that are not simply pragmatic. Those capable of enforcement in this way include some aspects of the right to just conditions of work, to safe and healthy working conditions, to reasonable notice before termination of employment, to organise, to bargain collectively and the right of children and young persons to protection (Hepple 1987 p 87).

In essence, Hepple is suggesting that a Community plinth of social rights could be established simply on the basis of a ruling from the European Court of Justice. If the Court were to make such a ruling it would be tantamount to establishing a European Social Constitution with far-reaching implications. In particular, if a European Social Constitution were established in this way then the various employment and labour rights would probably have direct applicability. As a result, interest groups in the member states would be able to challenge aspects of national labour law or call into question specific practices of individual companies which they regarded as breaching the Constitution. This type of behaviour would be similar to the actions of equal opportunities groups in relation to Community equality laws. Thus a Social Constitution could cause a proliferation of opportunistic European strategies on the part of interest groups which occasionally use Community law and institutions as an extra, third level to reinforce or improve their national position.

Another implication of adopting a European Social Constitution would be to give the European Court of Justice a more central role in social policy, since it would presumably have the task of deciding whether or not a social right had been breached by a member state or a company. The Court of Justice played a key role in extending EC social legislation, particularly EC equality legislation, during the 1980s, when a political impasse existed in this field. If its role in these cases is anything to go by, then the Court of Justice will ensure that social rights are implemented properly.

Of course, if national interest groups bring cases before the Court of Justice in the hope of obtaining favourable rulings, the formal political decision-making process becomes less important to the operation and direction of social policy. Certainly the ability of a single member state to bring social policy developments effectively to a halt by continually vetoing proposals, as was the case with the British Government, would be undermined. Thus a European Social Constitution would, in all likelihood, precipitate a root-and-branch change to Community social policy. Small wonder that the Thatcher administration baulks at the idea. It would raise a political storm of Herculean proportions if such a Constitution were established.

A Social Régime

Whether a Social Constitution or something equivalent will be established is still open to question. Within the Community, when controversial or potentially divisive proposals are made, the first response is to try to construct a compromise solution (Hurwitz 1988). Thus, faced with the possibility of deep political divisions over the Social Constitution proposal, the Economic and Social Committee — the Community's main consultative forum — produced a report, known as the Beretta Report which suggested a possible way to avoid a clash on the issue.

The Beretta Report

Specifically, the Beretta Report proposed that the Community should establish a Charter of Social Rights which would be 'exemplary' in character rather than having a legally binding status. To use more formal language, the Beretta Report was suggesting that the social dimension to the 1992 project should take the form of a 'régime' rather than a 'constitution'. The term 'régime' is borrowed from the literature on international political economy where it has been defined as 'sets of implicit or explicit principles, norms or rules, decision making procedures' (Krasner 1983, p 2). Within this definition the plinth of social rights would constitute a social régime which would comprise more than guidelines but less than legally binding obligations. Broadly, they would have the same status as a Recommendation — a form of political decision that the European Council can adopt which, although it has no formal legally binding status, imposes an informal moral obligation on the member states to take some action in the relevant area.

Obstacles to a social régime

For a Community social régime to operate in a manner conceived by the Beretta Report and its supporters, it will have to surmount some fairly formidable obstacles. The most immediate obstacle is whether it will receive the support of the current British Government. On paper, the Thatcher administration should be able to live with the social régime approach since it is a much weaker alternative to the Social Constitution proposals and would not impose any direct legal constraints on commercial enterprises. But so great is the opposition of the British Government to any proposals which even hint at disturbing the free workings of markets, or which could be construed as giving the Community a permanent presence in the European labour market, that its assent to the initiative is far from assured.

Before it can become fully operational, a social régime must also get the active support of the employers. In all probability, the employers would have little difficulty in agreeing to the creation of norms or conventions for the European labour market if these had the same status as the OECD's code of conduct for transnational corporations, or even as the Community's code of conduct for European companies with investments in South Africa. But presumably the supporters of a European social régime would not be satisfied with such an arrangement, for most of the evidence suggests that these non-binding international arrangements have only a marginal impact on the policies and behaviour of governments and companies (Blanpain 1984, Holland 1985).

Ideally its supporters would like to see a social régime which would require some type of ongoing institutional engagement, an 'institutional place' in Eurojargon, between the social partners and possibly even the Commission and the member states. Such a régime would have four aims:

(1) To monitor and assess the extent to which the 'exemplary' plinth of social rights is being observed by the member states and commercial organisations
(2) To attempt to extend the remit of the régime by agreeing to new principles which could be added to the plinth
(3) To draw up operational guidelines for the implementation of the informal social rights
(4) To maintain direct links with national institutions and arrangements for collective bargaining so as to facilitate the rapid transfer of information on industrial relations

developments between the member states, and to exhort these bodies to act on agreed Community labour market policies

A Community social régime along these lines would be very different from the OECD's guidelines for transnational companies or any other current international labour arrangement.

The Social Régime in Practice

Employee involvement

Two concrete examples may give the reader a better understanding of how a social régime may work in practice. Consider the issue of worker/employee participation. The idea that Community-wide forms of participation should be established was first proposed in 1972. At that time, the proposal drawn up by the Commission was for the codetermination system that operates in West Germany and the Netherlands to be established by the other member states. However, this proposal was rejected out of hand largely because it totally ignored the diversity in institutional relationships between management and labour that existed throughout the Community. After more than a decade of seemingly endless negotiations, a revised and modified proposal for participation came before the member states. The new proposal, which would apply to companies with 1,000 workers or more, set out two alternative participation systems under a two-tier board model and a single-tier board model from which companies could choose. But, as the proposal was seen as being too complex and too imprecise to allow the easy implementation of any of the alternatives, it too was rejected by the member states.

In the context of 1992 a new and more closely-defined version of the participation proposal has been put forward by the Commission. The main change it introduces is the insertion of an additional 'negotiated' model of participation. Under this model, management and labour would not have to adjust to a preordained system of participation, but could devise their own arrangement provided it included some basic features (eg that information is exchanged on company investment and employment plans, that formalised meetings occur between employers and employees and that the arrangement has been formally negotiated with the employees). The purpose of inserting the third model was to allay the concern of British businesses that they would have to introduce 'continental' style worker-participation institutions. The negotiated model will allow them to build on the expansion of communication and consultation that has occurred in recent years in British industry.

In real terms, the new proposal will not require any radical changes in participation and consultation arrangements in European industry. As a result, the revised proposal, which will take the form of a Directive, has a better chance of being adopted by the European Council than earlier drafts. In terms of a social régime, the significance of this initiative is twofold.

In the first place, it creates a bottom line as regards Community-wide participation and consultations: most workers, with the exception of those employed in smaller enterprises, will have the right to information and consultation. But at the same time, the initiative has sufficient flexibility to allow some companies and countries to develop more advanced forms of participation than others. It is a recognition of *Europe plusieurs vitesse* — a Europe of different speeds — in the employment and labour field.

Secondly, the use of the legislative machinery is not altogether ruled out under the social régime model, but can be used to establish a framework within which companies and countries can choose from a series of options. Some options will not deviate significantly from their existing practice.

The introduction of new technologies

The joint opinion from the Val Duchesse New Technologies Working Party may be used as another example of how the social régime should work in practice. The Working Party suggested, among other things, that companies should adjust their information and consultation procedures, as well as their training, so that new technologies could be introduced in a socially-responsible (and commercially-efficient) manner. If the social régime was operating properly, these suggestions would be placed, more or less automatically, on the collective bargaining agendas at the member state level for employees and trade unions to discuss. The logic of the arrangement is that the European social dialogue would concentrate on policy principles and goals, whereas the methods of implementing these principles would be discussed at a national level. The problem of the institutional diversity in industrial relations arrangements between the member states would, therefore, be circumvented.

However, because of their reluctance to become involved in any type of process which could lead to European collective bargaining it is doubtful whether the employers would support this type of arrangement. If the Community is to avoid having a decentralised social régime or a weak and hollow version of an active social régime, then the Commission and other member states which are becoming more committed to an interventionist social dimension to the 1992 programme, will have to persuade or force the British Government and the European employers' organisations to change their minds.

Chapter 5
European Collective Bargaining

Introduction

As equally contentious an issue as the adoption of a Community social legislation, is that of some form of collective bargaining between trade unions and employers on a European level.

The idea of European forms of collective bargaining first emerged as a concrete strategic option in the late 1960s and early 1970s. The biggest influences in its favour came from a large section of trade union opinion and the European Commission. Either as a result of the resurgence of class conflict or through being incorporated within a dense network of national economic decision-making structures, trade unions found themselves in a much stronger position throughout western Europe at that time (Crouch and Pizzorno 1978). With the increase of their authority came a desire to open up new dimensions of activity and to extend their presence in previously weak and even uncharted areas (Levinson 1972).

One key area requiring redress was the position of trade unions *vis-à-vis* multinational corporations which had mushroomed within the European economy during the 1960s. To establish trade unions as a genuinely countervailing power to the multinationals, a strategy of setting up combine committees, involving trade union representatives from different countries in Europe working for the same multinational corporations, was developed (Ulman 1975).

At the same time, the European Commission was becoming concerned that the Community was getting bogged down with implementing essentially 'negative' policies to remove trade barriers and other restrictive practices among the member states. To help improve its technocratic and faceless image, the Commission proposed that the Community should strengthen its links with the European trade union and employer organisations by incorporating them within the institutional and decision-making structure operating in Brussels (Kirchner 1980). Through their incorporation it was hoped that the social partners might develop a 'European' outlook, and thereby might help to give the Community a 'human' face.

These two relatively distinct influences (one from the trade unions and the other from the Commission) ensured that pressure for European collective bargaining operated both at the horizontal (company) level and vertical (institutional) level. While no coherent or fully worked out form of collective bargaining emerged at either level, more significant developments occurred in the vertical sphere. Probably the main reason for this was the existence of trade union and employer organisations at the European level which facilitated interaction between them and the Commission (Sargent 1986 and 1987).

The Social Partners at the European Level

The main employer organisation at the Community level is the Union of Industrial and Employers' Confederations of Europe (UNICE) (CEC 1978). This organisation, formed in 1958 (the same year as the Common Market was created), is the European equivalent of the British Confederation of British Industries (CBI). Its main functions are to lobby and attempt to influence the decisions of Community institutions as well as to provide members at the national level with information on Community affairs.

Alongside UNICE there exists a number of sector level employer organisations. An unwritten agreement ensures that while UNICE does not comment or make policy on specific industrial or commercial matters, the sector employer organisations stay clear of issues which are of general concern for employers. In comparison with European trade unionism, relatively little has been written about European employers and how they represent their interests at the Community level. To a large extent, this is the result of UNICE being able to resolve differences between affiliates in a relatively effective

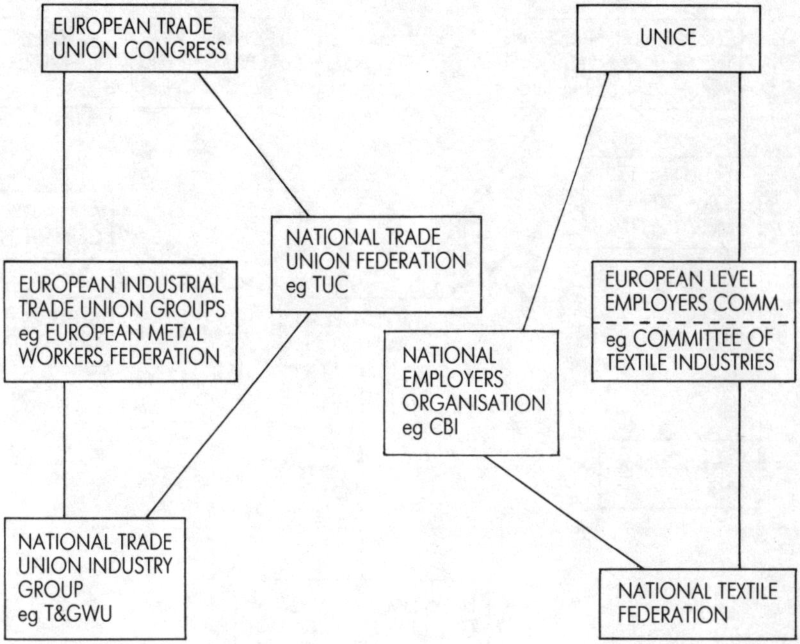

Figure 1 **Social partners at the European level**

and quiet manner and by its tendency not to initiate but to respond to Commission or trade union proposals.

The trade union equivalent of UNICE is the European Trade Union Confederation (ETUC). This organisation was formed in 1973, bringing together a number of different trade union bodies which had been operating at the Community level since the early 1960s. Before 1973 the European trade union organisations were highly fragmented, being split on religious and ideological grounds (Teague 1984). However, as a result of the influences of regionalism, détente and the multinationals, these separate trade union organisations decided to dissolve themselves and form a single federation named ETUC (Roberts and Liebhieberg 1976).

At the same time wholesale reorganisations to European

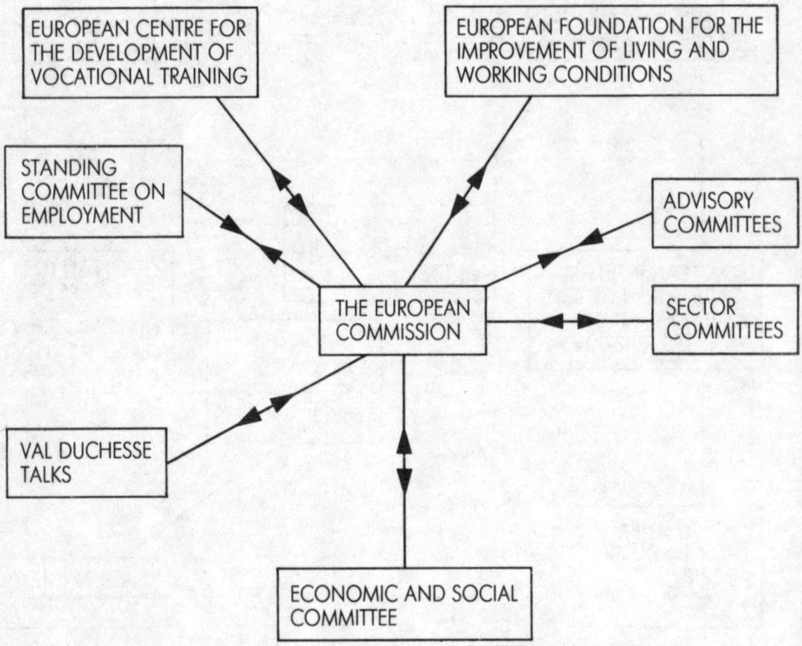

Figure 2 **The Community's institutional structure for social policy**

trade union industrial committees took place in the early 1970s. Like the industrial employer groups, the trade union organisations are primarily concerned with labour affairs at the sector level (Kirchner 1980). The expectation was that the reorganisations would result in the emergence of a new streamlined and effective European trade union structure (Baranouin 1986).

The Social Partners and the Community's Institutional Structure for Social Policy

In an effort to increase the Community's links with trade unions and employers, the Commission proposed several institutional and organisational initiatives. In the first place, between the mid-1960s and the early 1970s the Commission set up a number of sector committees composed of equal numbers of management and labour representatives with Commission officials in attendance in a purely administrative capacity.

Table 7 **The Joint Sector Committees (and date of establishment)**

Committee	Date of Establishment
(1) Joint Committee on Social Problems of Agricultural Workers	1963
(2) Joint Committee on Social Problems in Sea Fishing	1968
(3) Joint Advisory Committee on Social Problems in Road Transport	1965
(4) Joint Advisory Committee on Social Problems in Inland Navigation	1967
(5) Rail Transport Committee	1971
(6) Joint Committee on the Harmonisation of Working Conditions in the Coal Industry	1955
(7) Joint Committee on the Harmonisation of Working Conditions in the Iron and Steel Industry	1955
(8) Joint Committee on the Footwear Industry	1971 (suspended in 1982)

The purpose of these committees was described as 'to keep a watch on economic and social developments in their sectors, seek to conclude collective bargaining agreements and submit proposals for Community action to institutions' (Cripps 1987 p 54).

Clearly the Commission had high expectations for these committees, wanting them to help construct a European system of collective agreements and to contribute to the formation of Community industrial and labour market policies for the sectors. For the most part, however, the Committees have not lived up to these expectations. Only the sector committee covering agricultural workers was able to conclude a collective agreement. But as its provisions fell short of those already in place at the national level it was not considered to be very important (Robbins 1986). Unable to reach any concrete agreements or to make any policy proposals for their sectors, most of the committees lost their way by the late 1970s, meeting infrequently and discussing little of any substance.

In addition to establishing these sector committees, the Commission also sought to integrate the social partners within the Community's institutional framework by appointing them to the various advisory and sub-committees that existed to help formulate and implement EC social policy.

Advisory Committees in the social policy area

(1) Advisory Committee on Vocational Training
(2) Advisory Committee on Safety, Hygiene and Health Protection at Work
(3) Mines Health and Safety Committee
(4) General Committee for Health and Safety
(5) European Social Fund Advisory Committee
(6) Advisory Committee on Social Security — Migrant Workers
(7) Free Movement of Workers Advisory Committee

These committees were established for a variety of reasons. First, they were to advise on the implementation of particular policies. For example, the Mines Health and Safety Committee, made up of mining engineers from the member states, would provide the Commission with crucial information about the potential and limitations of certain policies. Secondly, and particularly relevant to the work of the European Social Fund, they were to further the structural policies of the Community. Thirdly, some of the committees, for example the Advisory Committee on Health, Hygiene and Health Protection at Work, were set up primarily to assist with the standardisation of laws in the different member states. Lastly, and more generally, the committees were expected to contribute to the development of EC social policy.

Largely because they do not have to initiate policy but merely respond to proposals drawn up by the Commission, both the trade unions and employers have been more comfortable in these committees and thus have played a more positive role.

The Nature of the Community's Social Policy Institutional Framework

The Commission's initiatives, along with other efforts at incorporating interest groups within the Community's decision-making process, have been viewed as an attempt at creating a corporatist system at the EC level (Sargent 1986). Corporatism normally implies the nation state taking a direct or influential role in economic and social affairs in an effort to obtain certain politically-determined goals (Cox 1988). Used in this sense, corporatism is an inappropriate term to explain the inclusion of the social partners within the Community's institutional structure, primarily because the EC has not got the equivalent capacity to intervene in these policy areas to influence pay settlements, inflation rates and employment levels (Wallace 1984).

Even if this problem is overlooked, the corporatist thesis still appears defective, since a key aspect of such a system is the willingness on the part of interest groups to participate fully in the arrangement, which may on occasion mean disciplining their members to accept its decisions (Hayward 1986). Neither of these ingredients was present in the Community's institutional structures for labour and industrial affairs: the employers are unwilling to enter into European agreements and no Community-level interest group organisation has the capacity to bind its national affiliates to any decisions emanating from EC committees.

The incorporation of the social partners within the Community institutions is perhaps better understood in the context of the dynamics of European integration. From the late 1960s, the Commission has been concerned with increasing the legitimacy of the Community as an economic and social institution among the citizens of Europe. By increasing the role of the social partners in the decision-making process the Commission was hoping it would be able to extend its policy interventions in the labour and employment fields. In other words, establishing a dialogue between the trade unions and employers was a type of legitimation process intended to help the Community to establish a greater presence in labour market issues (Schmitter 1969). But it cannot be concluded that this process was in any way effective since the social partners play only a passive role in the Community's decision-making process.

Collective Bargaining on the Horizontal Terrain

Probably more disappointing than the Commission's institutional initiatives have been developments, or more precisely the lack of developments, at the horizontal level. When the European trade union structure was reorganised in the early 1970s it was assumed that extra-national collective bargaining would emerge as a matter of course inside multinational corporations (Windmuller 1980). But efforts made by the ETUC and the European trade union industrial committees to establish horizontal forms of collective bargaining or labour collaboration have produced few results. By late 1986 only a handful of agreements involving workers and management in some form of extra-national dialogue had been concluded. The agreement covering the trade unions in two European multinationals — Thompson Grand Public and BSN — is produced in Appendix 3. More recently, two similar agreements have been concluded with two multinationals — Continental Can and Honeywell Bull (Northrup *et al.* 1988).

Other attempts have been made to increase European trade union collaboration outside the official structure. For example, on several different occasions local government administrations in the member states have combined to help organise and support extra-national forms of action by trade unions. Thus, in the early 1980s the municipal governments in London and Paris were largely responsible for the trade unions employed in plants owned by the American multinational Kodak in each region getting together to fight the company's European restructuring plan (Wainwright 1987). With the local administrations providing financial, personnel and political support, the unions were able to coordinate a highly professional and effective campaign leading to the company significantly revising and modifying its initial intentions.

In another initiative, local authorities in regions where the economies are dominated by the car industry have organised a series of conferences and workshops with the aim of getting the respective trade unions to formulate a European labour strategy for the industry. While such initiatives are to some extent path-breaking, they remain for the most part the exception. Horizontal trade union action in Europe is still very much a concept rather than a reality (Haworth and Ramsay 1987).

Why did European (horizontal) collective bargaining not emerge?

The economic environment

Overall, the gap between early expectations and subsequent developments as regards European collective bargaining appears discouragingly large. Why did European collective bargaining not emerge?

Three factors largely account for why no meaningful movement has occurred in this direction:

- The deep economic recession experienced by most European countries since the mid-1970s.
- The opposition from employers.
- The shortcomings in the trade unions themselves.

Economic crisis

Each is discussed in turn. Support for European, and even international, collective bargaining reached an apex when Western economies were still fairly prosperous and when the trade unions at that time were in a secure position in most member states of the Community. In this environment the trade unions had sufficient latitude to address the question of how to build an effective countervailing power to the multinationals.

With the advent of the economic crisis, the situation changed radically. Instead of discussing the possibilities of European labour strategies, trade unions became preoccupied with defending their members' jobs at the national level in the face of major redundancies and rationalisation programmes. Frequently, this defensive action amounted to trade unions from different nation states trying to persuade multinationals to transfer their closure programmes to another country (Lange *et al.* 1982 and Gourevitch *et al.* 1984): hardly an environment conducive to the forging of international trade union links!

Employer resistance

Another factor hindering the emergence of European collective bargaining has been the strong resistance of employers either to collective bargaining across national boundaries in Europe or to a formal Community institutional arrangement involving management and labour. By and large employer organisations have been successful, certainly more successful than the unions, in defending their interests at the European level. Thus, for example, the Commission has been unable to get the member states to agree to any proposals for labour legislation which are strongly opposed by employers. To give some insight into how the employers have proved more capable of ensuring that their view prevailed over that of the trade unions, it is worth comparing how both responded to a piece of proposed labour legislation — the draft Vredeling Directive.

The social partners and the draft Vredeling Directive

The popularly known draft Vredeling Directive was an attempt by the Commission to give legislative expression to the trade union demand that workers in multinational corporations should have formal information and consultation rights (Blanpain 1983). From the very outset the employers were extremely hostile to the Vredeling proposal, regarding it as the thin edge of the wedge leading to full-blown international collective bargaining.

UNICE's objections were based on four main points:

(1) The Commission had not proved the need for an EC Directive in this field, especially as most multinationals keep within the OECD guidelines.

(2) The Treaty of Rome did not provide the legal basis for the Directive.
(3) EC enterprises might be jeopardised in competing with firms from non-member states if a stricter law was created in the Community and not in other countries elsewhere in the world.
(4) As the Directive was an attempt to convert OECD and International Labour Organisation (ILO) recommendations into EC law it would interfere with existing international instruments.

Action by UNICE

To win support for its views, UNICE launched a major action programme, involving the recruitment of public relations and lobbying experts inside and outside the Community. Alongside UNICE's campaign, industrial relations experts and lawyers working for US multinationals as well as representatives from the four largest American trade organisations — the National Association of Manufacturers, the US Council for International Business, the US Chamber of Commerce, and the National Foreign Trade Council — formed a committee with the sole purpose of lobbying against the Vredeling proposal (Community Markets April 1983). This committee organised numerous high-level delegations to Brussels and other European capitals to win support for its position. In addition, the Japanese employers' organisation, Keidansen, warned Ivor Richards, the Social Affairs Commissioner in the early 1980s, that Japanese companies might reduce their investments in the Community if the Vredeling proposal was adopted (Community Markets July 1983). Plainly multinational corporations, no matter what their country of origin was, felt threatened by this initiative.

Inside the Community UNICE urged its members to take effective action against the proposal. So, although the proposed Directive was not far removed from German law and practices, the German employers' federation declared that it 'categorically' rejected the need for such a piece of Community legislation. In Britain, like in other member states (most notably Italy and Denmark), the main employers' organisation, the CBI, urged its members to introduce or strengthen consultative arrangements in order to weaken the case for the Directive.

To give weight to its campaign, the CBI surveyed its top 836 members to see the extent to which they had consultative procedures. The findings of the survey, which the CBI conceded were not representative, suggested that not only did companies have some form of consultative mechanism but also that the majority had recently strengthened or improved these provisions. The message being presented by the CBI was clear: as consultation was already widespread in industry there was no requirement for Community legislation in the area. The CBI used the results of the survey in its campaign against Vredeling, which involved extensive lobbying of MEPs, MPs, government officials and so on (CBI 1986). Thus, opposing the Vredeling proposal was a high priority for the business community.

Counter-action by the ETUC

For its part, ETUC also launched a major publicity and lobbying campaign, but in support of the Directive. An information pamphlet was produced which it hoped would be distributed on shop floors across Europe. The basic strategy was to create what the ETUC called a 'general awareness of the possibilities of the Directive' (ETUC 1982) and to win solid support at worker level. Through such ground-level support, the ETUC hoped that wavering member states and politicians would be brought into line behind the draft Directive. ETUC also relied on sympathetic Commissioners and Commission officials for support. Unlike the employers, however, the ETUC could not enlist the support of their counterparts from countries outside the Community: the statement by the Japanese employers warning of an investment strike could not be matched by Japanese trade unions. Moreover, the trade unions could not muster the same resources as the employers for their lobbying and campaigning activities. A *Sunday Times* reporter captured this point vividly when covering the European Parliamentary debate on Vredeling: he said,

> On Tuesday taxis swept up to the Parliament building bearing the most formidable galaxy of professional lobbyists Strasbourg has seen ... the union lobby consisted of a couple of pleasant individuals from the European TUC handing out leaflets (*Sunday Times* October 11th 1983)

To supplement its activity at the European level, the ETUC called on its affiliates to launch campaigns on the issue within the member states. But in Britain, at least, the TUC failed to undertake any meaningful activity. In fact, the TUC's action on the Vredeling proposal amounted solely to producing an information briefing for individual British trade unions and a submission to a British Government consultative exercise on the issue (Interviews with TUC officials). Contrasted with the CBI's highly visible and active campaign, this was a poor showing on the part of British trade unions. This response however was not primarily caused by indifference, but was largely a result of the trade unions being occupied with other priorities, namely, opposing the introduction of national legislation aimed at reducing trade union immunities and the implementation of a series of major redundancy programmes in both the private and public sectors (Crouch 1986). This point reinforces conclusions made elsewhere in the book that unless the national climate is favourable for trade unions, it is unlikely that they will become actively engaged on European issues (Teague 1989a).

The picture that clearly emerges is that the employers were more organised and effective in representing their interests than the trade unions. This assessment concurs with the views of some trade union leaders. In his address to a conference on multinational companies, Herman Rebhan, the General Secretary of the International Metalworkers Federation said, 'We have to be honest and say that the multinational companies beat us to the mark in the battle over the Directive' (Rebhan 1985). The lesson he draws from the episode is that the trade unions must learn to become more effective 'manipulators' of the European bureaucracy.

Limitations to European trade unions

A third factor contributing to the inch-like progress towards European collective bargaining has been certain organisational and political shortcomings on the part of trade unions themselves. Although it was widely accepted by the European trade unions when ETUC was established that their fragmented regional structure needed to be unified, sharp differences of opinion existed over the exact role and functions of that new body. One view, held by appointed ETUC officials and some continental trade unions, was that over time the powers and authority of ETUC should increase so as to place it in a better position to enter into European collective bargaining arrangements. A past President of ETUC expressed this viewpoint when he suggested that the creation of ETUC 'would mean the member confederations gradually transferring their national sovereignty' (ETUC 1979).

Opposing official union outlooks

An opposing outlook held by the British TUC among others, was that the main role of ETUC was to assist national collective bargaining efforts by researching the activities of multinationals and by disseminating information on industrial relations developments among countries. One report of a speech made by a British trade union delegate at an ETUC Conference aptly captured the thrust of this approach:

> He also expressed the view that central international collective bargaining was not necessary to counter the power of multinational employers as was suggested in the action programme, and he suggested that the ETUC might assist by ensuring that practical information about industry throughout Europe was available to workers on the shop floor, that advice was available to national centres regarding possible legislative action to control multinational companies and that the ETUC should ensure that their activities were directed towards meeting the practical needs of officials and unions (TUC 1975 p 222).

Clearly the TUC considered there to be limits to European trade unionism.

'Maximalist' and 'minimalist' positions

This difference of view between what can be termed 'maximalist' and 'minimalist' positions has resulted in a number of tensions and even open divisions, hampering the work of trade union bodies at the Community level. For instance, in their eagerness to revamp completely the European structure, the maximalists attempted, not only to make the previously independent trade union industrial committees subsidiaries of the ETUC, but also to impose fairly strict conditions on how they were to organise and operate. As a result of this move, an internal dispute erupted inside the ETUC which lasted for more than two years. Although the dispute cannot be regarded as major, it was sufficiently important to divert ETUC officials from other more constructive activities (Baranouin 1986).

The minimalists also caused their share of problems. For instance, in the early 1980s there was considerable ill feeling between the British TUC and some continental union federations over the former's opposition to Great Britain's membership of the Community (Teague 1989b). To the continental unions the TUC's stance of wanting to play a pivotal role inside the ETUC, while being unequivocally opposed to Community institutions, seemed highly inconsistent and opportunistic.

These and other disputes undermined the ability of the ETUC to develop well-thought-out and coherent proposals. On one occasion the TUC and the German DGB openly clashed on the merits or otherwise of exchange and import controls in a tripartite meeting also involving the employers and the Commission. Such embarrassing episodes hardly enhanced the reputation of European trade unionism. But fortunately for the trade unions, policy coordination has become better in recent years, largely as a result of the high-quality research work conducted by the European Trade Union Institute.

Lack of resources

Another practical factor limiting the effectiveness of European trade union organisation is the lack of financial and personnel resources. For example, the European Metal Workers Federation, once described by a sympathetic observer as heralding a new form of working class internationalism (Barratt-Brown 1977), is staffed by only a handful of people, who can do little more than the administrative tasks necessary to keep the organisation functioning. The problem of lack of resources, coupled with the differences over strategy and policy mentioned above, has resulted in many of the European trade union industrial committees losing their way, servicing neither the needs of trade unions at the horizontal level nor making an effective input into the institutional structure of the Community (Interviews with European Commission officials).

The interaction of these three factors prevented any meaningful or sustained form of European collective bargaining emerging during the late 1970s or early 1980s. So few were the developments in this area that European collective bargaining, or at least forms of trade union/employer collaboration in the European context, became virtually written off as an idea which had had its day. Yet in recent years, the idea of involving the trade unions and employers in the Community decision-making structure has been revised and is once again back on the agenda. The Delors's plan to establish a social dialogue at the European level can be seen as an attempt to rehabilitate this idea. Moreover, there is even talk of reviving the flagging sector committees so that a 'frank exchange of views' can take place at the European industry level between the social partners. But, as the analysis of these two arrangements shows, the outlook appears bleak for any meaningful trade union/employees collaboration at the Community level. The main stumbling block is the attitude of employers, since they remain opposed to, or at least unconvinced of the need for, any arrangement being established at the Community level which could be interpreted or construed as European collective bargaining. Employers in almost every member state are now pressing for more decentralised company level industrial relations where national influence on collective bargaining outcomes would be kept to a minimum. In this situation, it is unlikely that they will voluntarily agree to participate in a Community-level forum which aims to influence the labour market behaviour of companies.

Developments at the Horizontal Level

The current wave of Europeanisation has also lead to more optimistic assessments about the possibilities of horizontal action involving the social partners, particularly the trade unions. With only little evidence to support the feasibility of their case, several authors have recently argued for greater trade union horizontal action in Europe (Palmer 1987, Coates and Topham 1986, Coates 1986). To a large extent, this type of action is seen as a possible way to compensate for the decline of trade union power at the national state level. In this respect, their books differ from earlier writings on the subject which regarded international trade union action as building on the strength of labour in separate countries. Moreover, a wider range of activities than simply combined committee action is envisaged as being possible. Thus, for example, Palmer suggests that trade unions should join with other social groups to organise European campaigns in defence of welfare rights and provisions, employment and so on. Essentially, what is being suggested is that the trade unions should help create European social movements much in the mould of the European peace movement in the early 1980s and undertake similar type agitational action (Teague 1985).

It is questionable whether European trade unions should attempt fully to emulate the strategies and tactics of groups like the peace movement. As Offe (1987) has pointed out, interest groups in the latter category emphasise the principled and non-negotiable nature of their demands which are frequently illustrated by terms such as 'never' or 'ban'. Moreover, such groups tend to shun most forms of institutional incorporation, preferring instead direct forms of action like demonstrations. While trade unions on occasions get involved in this type of activity, good reasons exist why the *modus operandi* of trade unions in European affairs should not be limited to such initiatives.

To adopt such a stance would more or less confine European trade unions to reactive and defensive forms of action. Almost by definition the interaction with Community institutions to influence policy would take second place. Although the situation for trade union action within the Community's decision-making process is unfavourable, there is little evidence to show that it is any better in the horizontal arena. A few examples, like the Kodak case, can be invoked in support of horizontal action, but many more other examples can be cited where this approach has failed.

Just-in-time systems

It could even be argued that some features of the new international commercial environment have reduced the need for trade union collaboration across national boundaries. Consider the example of the just-in-time production system. In an effort to cut costs and remain competitive, many multinationals have established complex international production chains in which plants in individual countries are assigned particular tasks. While this just-in-time system increases efficiency, it has the built-in limitation that if one link in the chain is knocked out the entire system is jeopardised. On paper at least, this vulnerability gives trade unions increased scope for leverage of multinationals at the national level. Thus, for example, in 1988 British trade unions gained major concessions from the Ford motor company in an industrial dispute precisely because their strike action was threatening the company's international just-in-time system. Under this type of production system then, trade unions do not have to be concerned with developing international strategies to defend their interests. Obviously the argument should not be taken too far, as just-in-time systems at the international level are still not widespread.

Overall then the evidence suggests that the trade unions should have a pragmatic approach to horizontal forms of European trade union action: from their point of view there will be circumstances and occasions in which it will be the correct strategy to follow and others in which it will not. But, in the present economic and commercial climate, it may be worth while for the trade unions to lower their expectations about the potential gains from horizontal action. For instance, instead of seeking some form of collective bargaining at the international level, trade unions could try to persuade multinationals to extend the present consultation and communication boom within companies to incorporate international issues. Thus, despite the current optimism in some trade union circles, it is hard to escape the conclusion that horizontal trade union action will not be able to constitute a fully-fledged European labour strategy nor compensate for the relative decline of trade unions within the nation states.

Towards Opportunistic Europeanism

From a trade union point of view this is a fairly bleak assessment of the short to medium term prospects for European collective bargaining. Without a sustained upturn in economic fortunes and a more cooperative attitude on the part of the employers, it is unlikely that any meaningful or far-reaching new developments will occur in either the vertical or horizontal terrains. To the trade unions this situation must be very depressing. Realising that all is not well, some trade unions are beginning to reassess their conventional approach to Europe with a view to developing new strategies. One new line of thought is for trade unions to adopt an opportunistic European approach which would essentially involve using Community institutions and legislation as a 'third level' body to reinforce or improve their position within the nation state.

The closest example of this kind of behaviour in Britain is the European Community activities of single issue interest groups like the Equal Opportunities Commission (EOC) and the Child Poverty Action Group. Faced by what they regard as retrogressive legislation at home, these groups are increasingly turning towards Europe to see whether Community law can be exploited to defend and even further the interests of their constituencies. Thus, for example, it was the Equal Opportunities Commission which provided the financial backing and the legal expertise for Mrs Marshall when she took the case against Southampton Health Authority to the European Court of Justice. The Child Action Poverty Group provided similar support for Mrs Drake in her case against the Department of Health and Social Security. The Court of Justice rulings in both these cases obliged the British Government to make important changes to its domestic labour law (Brewster and Teague, Ch 7, 1989).

Exploiting the potential of European labour law is still very much in its infancy and the strategies pursued by the EOC etc are also at the experimental stage. Moreover, significant obstacles in terms of the complexity of European law and the processing of cases stand in the way of this type of action becoming common practice. Nevertheless, the trade unions are attracted to such an opportunistic European strategy for a number of reasons. For a start, pursuing this type of strategy circumvents many of the problems associated with vertical and horizontal forms of trade union action. For instance, as regards vertical action, the difficulties of getting the employers to participate meaningfully in a Community social arrangement, or of reconciling the divergent, and at times opposing, views of European trade unions are no longer important considerations. Similarly, the practicalities of launching effective horizontal action and campaigns are by-passed.

Furthermore, no opportunity costs are involved in pursuing opportunistic European strategies: attempts by the Commission to establish a social dialogue at the Community level are not compromised by national trade unions taking advantage of European law. Currently, the equality area is most open to opportunistic European strategies. In this area alone there are a whole range of employment practices and conditions which the trade unions could challenge. And if the current attempts at establishing a European Social Constitution succeed then the possibility opens up for similar types of strategy in other industrial relations areas.

Conclusions

It is clear from the above analysis that both benign and controversial aspects exist to the social dimension to the internal market. The free movement of workers, cooperation between national labour market institutions, and the European Social Fund can more or less be regarded as the benign policy areas. For the most part, policy formation and activity in these areas will be carried out in a relatively non-contentious and trouble-free environment. But, as the analysis also shows, some of the objectives and goals set in these three areas will not be easily met. If the member states are going to make any significant advances towards labour mobility inside the Community, then more resources are required on such matters as the mutual recognition of diplomas and training initiatives.

As regards cooperation initiatives, the Community needs to adopt a highly flexible and creative approach, for some of the issues that are being considered are not altogether amendable to cross-Community coordination. And in the Social Fund sphere, a good deal of uncertainty still remains about whether or not the new programme approach will be successful, as many of the operational specifics have yet to be worked out. Thus even though they can be regarded as benign, successful developments in these policy areas are far from assured in the context of 1992. Highly skilful policy work on the part of Community and national officials will be of significant importance.

The legislative and collective bargaining spheres are the controversial aspects of the social dimension to the 1992 programme. The extent to which the Community adopts a *dirigiste* or deregulated social dimension to the 1992 project will depend on the outcome of some hard political bargaining, if not total political confrontation between the maximalists, led by the Commission and perhaps Mitterrand, and the minimalists, led by the British Government and the European employer organisations. Given its past record of opposition to proposed EC social policies, the British government will not compromise easily on this issue.

At the same time, the European Commission and some of the member states who favour an interventionist social policy will also stand firm. They will be prepared to put up a fight to ensure that the 1992 programme is not reduced to a purely economic liberalisation programme. For they fully realise that, if there is one lesson to be learnt from the past 30 years of European integration, it is that to compromise too much with a minimalist point of view weakens integrative dynamics. For example, by compromising too readily with de Gaulle in 1965, the pro-European forces undermined the majority voting principle inside the Council of Ministers, thereby transforming the Community from an embryonic supernational institution into an intergovernmental body in which all decisions had to be reached on the basis of unanimity. The situation is currently so fluid that it is difficult to know which view will win the day. If the Commission or maximalist view prevails then a real attempt will be made to build an original extra-national labour market arrangement at the Community level. Such an arrangement would have a number of interrelated features or roles:

(1) *Facilitating role*
As a result of its ability to coordinate and initiate action across the member states, the Community will be in a key strategic position to facilitate the development of policy and measures involving interest groups and member states (eg taking action to facilitate an increase in labour mobility between the member states, or using its institutional arrangements to increase contact between interest groups, for instance equal opportunities interest groups, from the different member states).

(2) *Animating role*
This is linked to the above function. Again, because of its strategic location, the Community will be in the ideal position to transfer information between member states about particular employment and labour market policies which appear to be successful. In addition, it could even encourage member states to establish new and experimental projects on a wide range of topics.

(3) *Sponsoring role*
The Community will be able to use some of its own funds to sponsor employment and training measures which it considers a priority from a European point of view. For a considerable time to come, as we have seen, the lion's share of this money will go to the disadvantaged regions in the Community.

(4) *Strategic role*
In the industrial relations literature the term 'strategic action' on the part of the trade unions, employers and government is being used with increasing frequency. Essentially the term is referring to the need for all the actors in industrial relations systems to examine issues in a more forward-looking comprehensive way than is currently the case. The Community's social dialogue (if properly established) could play a crucial role in formulating new ideas and new approaches to problematical industrial relations and labour market matters. As the social partners at the Community do not engage in nitty-gritty exchanges over pay and working conditions, they are in an advantageous position to perform this role.

(5) *Enabling role*

The Community as a 'third level' institution represents another forum which national interest groups can use to further their interests. This could take a number of forms. It could take the form of the European trade unions getting together and organising a campaign to influence the Community to adopt a specific policy or programme. For example the trade unions may launch a European campaign to get a 35-hour week. Alternatively, it may simply involve a national interest group using European law in an effort to further its demands domestically.

(6) *Legislative role*

If the maximalist version, including the idea of a European social constitution, triumphs then the Community will have a much more direct relation to the nature and pattern of labour law in the member states. This may not involve the harmonisation of national industrial relations institutions and practices through which labour law is implemented, but it could involve a greater convergence of the content and type of such legislation. In a country like Britain, where law has traditionally played only a marginal role in industrial relations, this increased legislative role could lead to significant upheavals.

Traditionally, industrial relations systems have been regarded as comprising three institutional tiers: governments, employers and trade unions. At the top level, governments and other public institutions shape the socio-economic environment in which employers and trade unions operate and which directly intervene to regulate some aspects of industrial relations behaviour or practice. In the middle, there is some form of sector-level collective bargaining where employers and trade unions negotiate on rates of pay and other working conditions as well as devising a wide range of labour market and training programmes. The bottom tier largely consists of company-level personnel and employee relations, policies and issues. Although it is recognised that the importance of each tier varies across countries, it has been more or less assumed that no other factors have a determining influence on national industrial relations systems.

The adoption of the maximalist view would mean, to all intents and purposes, that a new, fourth industrial relations tier would be created at the European level. For by establishing a social dialogue between the social partners and extending EC employment legislation, an *economic and political opportunity structure* would be created at the European level through which the Community's presence is brought to bear more directly on labour market policies and practices in the member states.

Embedded in this opportunity structure would be the ideological principles of social cooperation and consensus which have governed the direction of industrial relations in 'continental' Europe since the Second World War. Policies pursued by the member states which contravene this approach — for example, those being enacted by the current Conservative Government — could be significantly moderated, if not undermined altogether, by trade unions using Community industrial relations laws and institutions. In the summer of 1988 Jacques Delors told the European Parliament that 'in 10 years, 80 per cent of economic and social legislation will originate in the EC'. If the above arrangement is established then Delors's vision may materialise.

An entirely different sequence of events would unfold if the Thatcher alternative prevails. The underlying rationale for this approach, which may be described as neo-liberal, is a particular view of why most Community countries have experienced high unemployment levels and a lack of new job opportunities in the past decade. Between the mid-1970s and the mid-1980s the Community lost 3 million net jobs, while in the same period the United States created 18 million net new jobs for a labour force about the same size as the EC's. The neo-liberal or Thatcher approach attributes the better job creation performance of the United States to the highly flexible nature of its labour market. By contrast, a wide ranging set of artificial inflexibilities and rigidities is seen to be responsible for the slowdown in the job generation process in Europe. The term 'Eurosclerosis' is used to capture this view of rigid markets and sluggish adjustments as the source of the Community's relatively weak performance.

More specifically, the Eurosclerosis thesis makes several arguments. In the first place, wages are too high and too rigid, resulting in workers being priced out of jobs. In addition, wage differentials are too small, hindering labour mobility and, as a result, structural adjustment. Furthermore, legally-based labour rights and employment protection schemes have gone too far, leading to high labour costs which in turn cause redundancies and discourage hiring. Finally, social security systems encourage voluntary unemployment and act as a disincentive to work. Trade unions and centralised bargaining arrangements are regarded as the main obstacles preventing wages adjusting to market conditions, while state intervention is held responsible for excessive legal and financial guarantees in labour markets and for limiting the power of trade unions so as to give employers more freedom of action in order to revive employment growth.

Working from this perspective, the current British Conservative Government has introduced wide ranging deregulatory labour market reforms. Now it wants the Community to follow suit. In practical terms this would mean that no social dialogue would be created at the European level and not only would there be no further European labour legislation, apart from that enacted in the health and safety fields, but also current Community social statutes would probably be streamlined.

The direction and texture of a minimalist social policy is summed up in the following quote by a French advocate:

> Let there be no mistake. The Europe of 1992 must be the Europe of Competition. Let us be vigilant and beware of Eurobureaucrats. We are currently kicking out bureaucracy and regulation from both our countries: we do not want to see them back through the Brussels door. We are reducing our tasks, our expenses, slimming down our administrations; we do not want to have a Europe with heavier institutions, heavier budgets, more European civil servants

> and rising taxes. Europe is a liberal area . . . it must not be a superstate following the pattern of the *dirigiste* nation states of the 1960s (Madelin 1988, p 103).

Thus, the arguments between the maximalists and minimalists about the content of a social dimension to the 1992 project are so intense because they involve two radically different models for the European labour market. Since the gap between these two models is so wide it is hard to see how a compromise solution can emerge. Some variant of the social régime proposal in which the Community has an indirect and informal influence over the European labour market may be a possible area where a compromise could be struck. But before that can happen, both sides will have to modify their views and be prepared to accept that they cannot fully obtain all that they would like. In other words, what appears to be at stake here is the depth of the new-found cooperation inside the Community.

If the various protagonists in the debate remain entrenched and adopt inflexible positions then this will be an indication that the bad old days of the late 1970s and early 1980s have not been left behind and that the new cooperative spirit is but a chimera. Conversely, if the member states adopt the cooperative route and attempt to reach a compromise deal then there may just be a possibility that the Community has entered a qualitatively new phase which will allow it to have a major influence on the direction of political and economic affairs in Europe.

APPENDICES

Appendix 1 The Decision-Making Framework of the EC

Before July 1987

The Community's decision-making process is outlined in Figure 3.

European Council and Council of Ministers

The Councils are made up of representatives from the member state governments, who safeguard national interests. Their role is to discuss and adopt policy legislation. They work mainly on the basis of consensus and unanimity so that effectively each state has a veto, though the Single European Act has introduced a measure of qualified majority voting.

European Commission

This is the executive arm of the Community, made up of civil servants and experts, divided into Directorates which deal with different subject areas. It has the power to initiate policy and legislation and to carry out decisions. It is intended to represent overall European interest.

European Parliament

The European Parliament has no power to pass legislation; it can only advise and consult. Its influence has grown since 1979, when its members (MEPs) were directly elected.

European Court of Justice

This is the Court of the Community, whose ruling are binding on all member states. It enforces and interprets the Treaty of Rome and all secondary legislation and has the power to hear cases directly and to give opinions on cases referred to it by national courts.

Social and Economic Committee

The Committee is made up of representatives from trade unions, employers and consumer interest groups. The committee must be consulted before

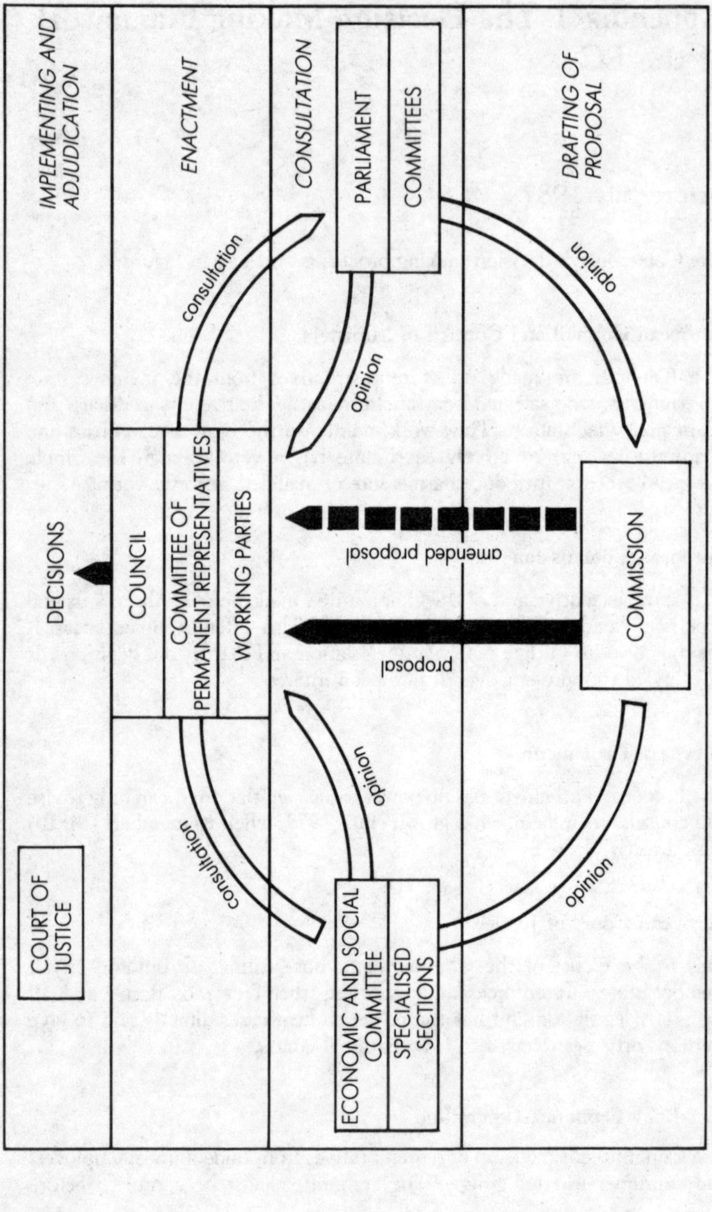

Figure 3 The Community's decision-making process

decisions are taken on a large number of subjects, and is also free to submit opinions on its own initiatives.

The Council of Ministers is the supreme decision-making body of the Community. Most of the decisions it currently takes are by unanimous voting, although, as detailed below, the Single European Act introduces some majority voting. The Council has the authority to issue Regulations, Directives, Decisions, Recommendations and Opinions. Regulations are of general application: they are binding in their entirety and applicable in all member states. Directives are binding on the member states to which they are addressed as regards the result to be achieved, but leave the form and methods of achieving it to the discretion of the national authorities. Decisions may be addressed to a government, a company, or a private individual: they are binding in their entirety on those to whom they are addressed. Recommendations and Opinions are not binding, though they do carry some 'informal' obligation.

When legally binding policies are made, the main responsibility for ensuring that they are fully implemented falls on the Commission. If the Commission considers that a member state has not properly enacted Community legislation, it can bring the country before the European Court of Justice. The Court of Justice, composed of eleven judges who are appointed for six years by agreement among the governments, ensures that the Treaties establishing the EC, and all subsequently secondary legislation (Regulations, Directives and Decisions), are implemented in accordance with the rule of law. Because secondary legislation is becoming more and more interwoven with the national law of individual member states, the Court has increasingly been called upon to give rulings on the applicability of Community statutes by national courts.

After July 1987

As noted in the text, the Single European Act was introduced to give the 1992 programme a legal base. As the Act changes the institutional framework to some degree, it may be worth while explaining its provisions in detail. The Act is a complicated and subtly-worded legal document, so it is necessary to break down the contents and place these under different headings: functional provisions; institutional reform; areas subject to the new decision-making structure; and other procedural and lesser changes.

Functional provision

The central functional provision of the Single European Act is the establishment of a completely liberalised internal market. Article 3A calls for this process to be completed by the end of 1992, and Article 100a (which replaces Article 100 of the Treaty of Rome that urges the approximation of national laws which affect the functioning of the Common Market) is the principal instrument for the accomplishment of this task. The Act outlines in considerable detail the actions that are necessary to establish a true internal market. These are summarised below. One of the central tasks is to achieve the harmonisation of indirect taxes. (Decisions of the Council of Ministers on this issue have to be taken on the basis of unanimity after consulting the European Parliament.)

The Act also allows the Council to adopt measures which 'approximate' national provisions in other areas. In particular, the Act permits the Council to introduce measures which allow for a high level of protection in the fields of health, safety, and environmental and consumer protection. Controls and restrictions are also imposed on member states unilaterally, introducing measures which affect imports. To assist the liberalisation of the internal market, the Council, taking account of the differences between economies, has to determine guidelines and conditions necessary to secure balanced progress. After 1992, the Commission is required to forward proposals for future action in the internal market.

Another key aspect of the Act is the strengthening of economic and social cohesion inside the Community by reducing regional disparities. To this end, the various sub-parts of Article 130 detail the methods to be used to reduce the backwardness of less-favoured regions, and instruct the Council, within a year, to revise and realign the rules of the various structural funds to meet the objectives.

A further functional area covered by the Act is technology policy and the environment. In the area of technology policy, the Act instructs the Council to establish multi-annual framework programmes, and in relation to the environment, it sets out a series of objectives and defines what action needs to be taken to meet them.

The only other significant part of the Act is that which gives formal recognition to the European Council and provides for European cooperation in the sphere of foreign policy.

Institutional reform

One important aspect of the Single European Act concerns the institutional revisions it introduces into the Community's decision-making process. The objectives of the revisions, known as the cooperation procedure, are to give the European Parliament an enlarged and more formalised role (although it does not give it any further rights or powers) and to introduce qualified majority voting into some areas of Community. The new cooperation procedure will work as follows:

The Council, acting by a qualified majority on a proposal from the Commission and after obtaining the opinion of the European Parliament, adopts a common position. Then the Council communicates that common position to the European Parliament (with a statement of reasons and of the Commission's position). If, within three months the European Parliament

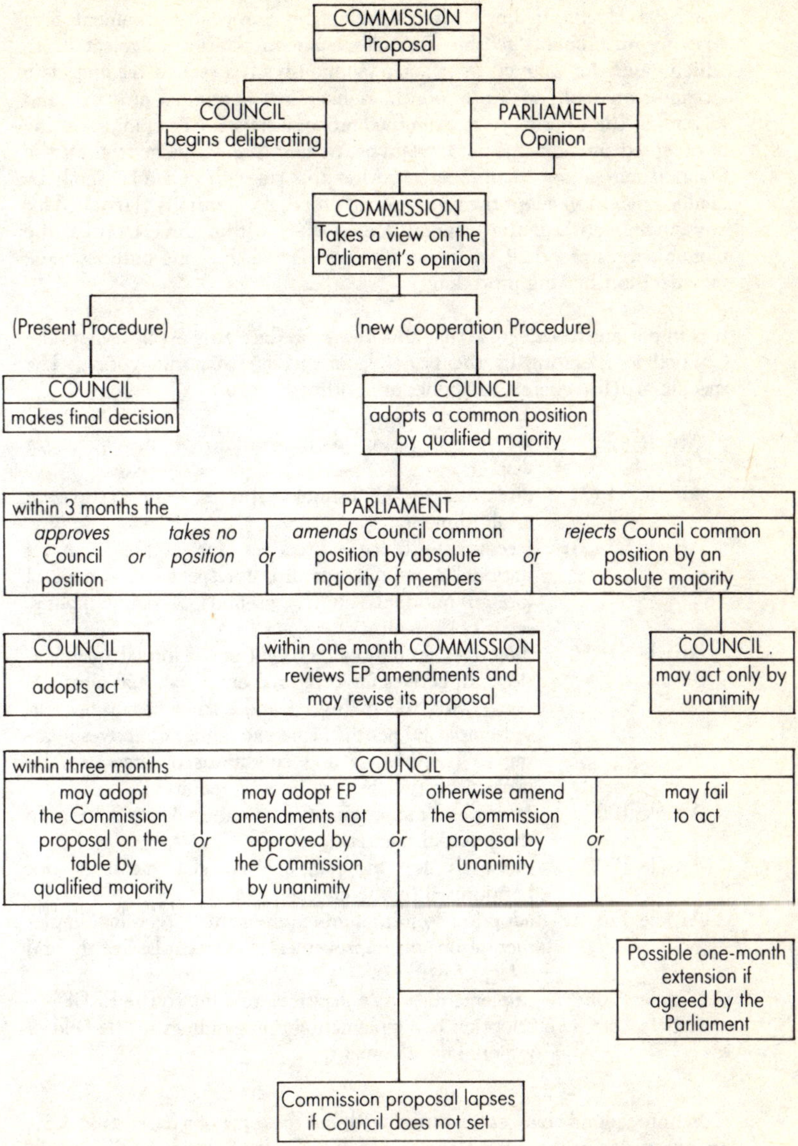

Figure 4 Flow-chart illustrating legislative process in the EC

approves the common position or takes no decision, the Council can act on the basis of that policy. Alternatively, the European Parliament may propose amendments to the Council's common position or reject it, in which case, the Council must act unanimously on a second reading. The Commission shall, within a month, re-examine its original proposals and forward to the Council its re-examined proposals (stating its opinion on any unaccepted amendments put forward by the European Parliament: these the Council may adopt unanimously). After this stage the Council shall, by qualfied majority, adopt the re-examined proposal (unanimity is required for any amendment). If the Council does not act within three months, the Commission's proposals are deemed to be rejected. Figure 4 outlines these new decision-making procedures.

It is important to recognise that this new procedure only applies where the Council is operating by the principle of qualified majority voting. The specific articles where this applies are outlined below.

Article 49:	measure to bring about freedom of movement for workers.
Article 54 (2):	directives for abolishing restrictions on freedom of establishment.
Article 56 (2):	(second sentence) directives for coordination of national measures providing for special treatment of foreign nationals on the grounds of public policy, security or health.
Article 57:	directives for mutual recognition of formal qualifications; directives for coordination of national measures concerning the taking up and pursuit of activities as self-employed persons; (but excluding) directives relating to training for and conditions of access to the professions (where unanimity is required).
Article 100A:	measures for approximation of national provisions as to the internal market.
Article 100B:	proposals for mopping-up national measures not harmonised by the end of 1992.
Article 118A:	adoption to minimum requirements for gradual implementation of improvements as regards health and safety of workers.
Article 130E:	implementation of decisions relating to the ERDF.
Article 130Q(2):	adoption of supplementary programmes in the field of regional development.

Other procedural changes are introduced, but these are of a lesser scale. One new provision makes minor changes to the Court of Justice so that it can hear 'certain classes of action brought by national or legal persons'. Under another revision the assent of the European Parliament becomes necessary for the admission of new member states and for the conclusion of certain international agreements.

Considerable confusion exists as to whether the Single European Act is a supranational or intergovernmental document. For instance, Mrs Thatcher has told the House of Commons that the Act does not undermine the Luxembourg Compromise to any great extent. Yet in Ireland the Supreme Court ruled that a referendum had to be held on the subject because the Act undermined national decision-making in the area of foreign affairs, and thereby jeopardised Irish neutrality. Probably, the Act is best viewed as making a number of statements of intent and objectives in various areas, some of which will involve majority voting. Thus, in the short term, it should not be interpreted as enforcing any significant transfer of political authority from the national to European sphere. But the changes it introduces will in all probability remove some of the legal and decision-making bottlenecks that have tied up the Community in recent years. As a result, the immediate impact on the Act will be the speeding-up of the Community decision-making process. Beyond that it is too early to make any other predictions.

Appendix 2 Geographical Breakdown of Social Fund Allocations

Table 1 **Training grants (£s) to local authorities**

Local authority	1981	1982	1983	1984	1985
Avon		19,946	98,239	977,371	1,125,989
Berkshire			108,137		
Borders				210,261	
Cambridgeshire				149,267	53,335
Cheshire		6,006	181,240	446,914	498,866
Cleveland	15,258	100,000	768,063	1,212,508	1,099,173
Clywd		29,600	232,929	22,323	546,836
Cornwall			56,531	662,562	1,190,585
Cumbria	51,217	59,406		59,791	64,593
Derbyshire			44,879	34,020	129,340
Devon	225,813		7,000	450,074	695,048
Dorset					8,498
Durham	47,044	65,550	142,235	102,368	202,522
Dyfred			173,093	121,324	467,458
Essex	80,849		105,230	243,599	339,072
Fife				4,738	395,837
Gloucestershire				80,284	57,617
Grampian				31,054	70,986
Greater London	153,517	815,420	1,516,636	2,906,598	5,662,229
Greater Manchester	70,617	3,822,603	362,832	8,647,404	3,853,834
Gwent			127,250	168,803	320,307
Gwynedd					51,911
Hampshire		15,000			12,767
Hereford & Worcester		467,500		50,776	260,735
Hertfordshire	51,000	81,225	63,380	469,904	154,129
Highland & Islands			202,450		590,288
Humberside				479,582	
Kent			32,320	50,760	29,773
Lancashire	9,256	13,935	617,411	553,318	2,822,893
Leicestershire	3,879	61,098	378,056		96,729
Lincolnshire				16,763	97,730
Lothian		112,927	262,239	2,762,851	2,905,367
Merseyside	214,590	1,276,170	1,637,865	3,964,378	6,736,215
Mid Glamorgan			147,908	12,500	666,016
Norfolk		51,348	106,067	17,396	31,256
North Yorkshire	36,225		38,005	3,640	80,143
Northamptonshire			142,200	262,658	35,950
Northumberland				71,479	409,086

Local authority	1981	1982	1983	1984	1985
Nottinghamshire		1,366,550		375,619	23,160
Powys				20,000	91,012
Salop			235,389	196,232	86,022
Somerset					110,721
South Glamorgan		22,082	56,250	34,345	206,758
South Yorkshire	32,238	50,284	1,035,335	938,263	2,746,532
Staffordshire	6,850	245,290	264,582	146,470	234,514
Strathclyde	138,085	297,727	3,172,799	3,532,164	7,938,498
Surrey				164,000	281,158
Tayside	12,000		736,565	384,645	419,486
Tyne & Wear	178,450	945,913	991,400	960,100	3,304,755
Warwickshire				125,249	353,745
West Glamorgan	45,875	232,696	28,550	140,705	
West Midlands	111,510	402,107	1,662,385	2,872,624	4,999,526
West Sussex				73,785	
West Yorkshire	636,041	806,459	2,188,693	2,326,686	6,875,585
Wiltshire				149,529	367,179

Table 2 **Employment grants (£s) to local authorities**

Local authority	1981	1982	1983	1984	1985
Cambridgeshire					185,964
Central			273,000	169,975	
Cheshire					
Cleveland	31,575	282,247	144,242	142,766	327,267
Clywd			50,000	4,968	117,167
Cornwall				344,760	79,479
Cumbria	809	34,990	70,543	78,000	75,503
Dumfries & Galloway		3,696		47,151	52,103
Durham	100,000	231,618	231,847	176,505	220,252
Dyfred			48,121	9,652	61,780
Fife					210,218
Grampian			100,974	13,500	
Greater Manchester	21,050	3,729,132	322,722	469,683	710,328
Gwent		78,000	152,507	205,060	
Gwynedd		10,882			
Highlands & Islands			189,150	53,000	203,388
Humberside			117,000	126,360	
Lancashire			4,624	12,675	41,061
Lincolnshire					11,823
Lothian			120,000	26,486	136,768
Merseyside	650,000	950,774	640,999	360,234	225,713
Mid Glamorgan	9,051	9,359	248,666	61,285	78,760
North Yorkshire				20,000	29,773
Northamptonshire				167,310	
Northumberland				20,420	
Nottinghamshire		48,750			

Local authority	1981	1982	1983	1984	1985
Salop			24,085	37,933	
South Glamorgan			5,359		
South Yorkshire	17,000	32,900	158,201	335,325	373,252
Staffordshire				32,651	7,215
Strathclyde		1,041,000	1,870,050	745,875	986,745
Tayside		507,000	250,000	55,575	107,672
Tyne & Wear	69,634	108,706	216,877	407,940	617,874
Warwickshire					24,811
West Glamorgan			56,880		402,323
West Midlands				58,283	610,756
West Yorkshire		202,762	66,193	207,006	225,963

Table 3

Local authority	1981	1982	1983	1984	1985
Cheshire				103,275	
Cleveland	66,325	133,425			
Devon	28,700				
East Sussex		96,000			
Essex				13,020	114,945
Gloucestershire				21,000	
Grampian		86,700			
Greater London	31,379	267,810	144,444		
Hampshire		18,500	26,900		
Highlands & Islands	49,500	48,750			
Lancashire				5,755	
Lothian	21,750	30,500	48,900		
Merseyside					4,978
Oxfordshire				23,500	
South Glamorgan		89,500			
Staffordshire		14,535			
Tayside			25,750		
Warwickshire		9,575			
West Midlands				45,067	126,585
West Yorkshire	27,600	3,900		144,270	
Yorks & Humberside				26,865	51,765

Table 4 **Employment grants to the different regions**

Region	1981	1982	1983	1984	1985
South East (Greater London)					
East Anglia					185,964
South West				344,760	79,479
West Midlands			24,085	10,408,981	10,052,260
East Midlands		48,750		167,310	11,823
Yorks & Humberside	17,000	235,662	341,394	9,438,084	8,375,745
North West	671,050	4,679,906	968,345	842,592	4,830,886
North	202,018	657,061	663,509	835,631	1,240,896
Wales	9,051	98,241	561,583	280,965	660,030
Scotland	1,524,696	2,803,174	1,098,062	1,696,894	

Table 5 **Grants for other social action to the different regions**

Region	1981	1982	1983	1984	1985
South East (Greater London)	31,379	382,310	404,094	36,520	114,945
East Anglia					
South West	28,700			21,000	
West Midlands		24,110		45,067	126,585
Yorks & Humberside	27,600	31,900		53,230	51,760
North West			51,755	108,253	
North	66,325	133,425			
Wales		89,500			
Scotland	71,250	165,950	74,650		

Table 6 **Training grants to the different regions**

Region	1981	1982	1983	1984	1985
South East (Greater London)	285,366	911,645	1,825,704	3,744,646	6,479,128
East Anglia		51,348	125,784	17,396	31,250
South West	225,813	19,946	161,770	2,170,291	3,188,458
West Midlands	118,310	1,114,897	2,162,356	38,660,656	21,777,326
East Midlands	3,879	1,397,648	565,135	838,327	436,244
Yorks & Humberside	704,504	856,743	3,554,304	28,777,326	18,893,882
North West	294,463	5,118,714	2,799,348	13,612,014	13,911,808
North	291,969	945,913	1,901,698	2,426,046	5,080,129
Wales	45,875	51,682	970,626	407,845	2,941,003
Scotland	150,085	410,654	4,374,063	6,925,574	12,320,462

Current UK Priority Areas Designated by the Commission

Counties (local authority areas):

Central, Cheshire, Cleveland, Clwyd, Cornwall, Derbyshire, Dumfries and Galloway, Durham, Dyfred, Fife, Greater Manchester, Gwent, Gwynedd, Hereford and Worcester, Highlands & Islands, Humberside, Isle of Wight, Lancashire, Lincolnshire, Lothian, Merseyside, Mid Glamorgan, Northumberland, Nottinghamshire, Salop, South Glamorgan, South Yorkshire, Staffordshire, Strathclyde, Tayside, Tyne & Wear, West Glamorgan, West Midlands, West Yorkshire.

Travel to work areas:

Workington (Cumbria), Coalville (Leicestershire), Corby (Northamptonshire).

Non-priority areas receiving Social Fund money:

Avon, Berkshire, Borders, Cambridgeshire, Devon, Dorset, East Sussex, Essex, Gloucestershire, Grampian, Greater London, Hampshire, Hertfordshire, Norfolk, North Yorkshire, Oxfordshire, Powys, Somerset, Suffolk, Surrey, West Sussex, Wiltshire, Warwickshire.

Appendix 3 Protocol Agreements (Thomson Grand Public)

Thomson Grand Public-European Metalworkers' Federation Liaison Committee

Taking into account the supranational character of the activities of the THOMSON GRAND PUBLIC Division, the signatories agree to set up a Liaison Committee, which will provide economic data on the industrial and trading situation with regard to THOMSON GRAND PUBLIC operations in Europe.

I-Composition

- The Managing Director of the firm THOMSON GRAND PUBLIC or his representative, together with the managers concerned.
- 15 representatives of trade unions organisations affiliated to the European Metalworkers' Federation (EMF)

II-Allocation of Seats

- 1 seat is reserved for a representative of the European Metalworkers' Federation.
- 14 seats are attributed to the representatives of trade union organisations affiliated to the EMF, or represented by the EMF, appointed from among the employees of this Division.

They are allocated as follows:

- 6 seats for the French organisations
- 4 seats for the German organisations
- 2 seats for the Italian organisations
- 2 seats for the Spanish organisations

III-Procedure

The Committee will meet every six months on THOMSON GRAND PUBLIC or EMF initiative, notice being given six weeks in advance.

The venue for the meeting will be chosen by THOMSON GRAND PUBLIC, which will meet all interpretation costs.

The travel and accommodation costs incurred by participants in these meetings will be met by the EMF.

All persons appointed who are employed in the THOMSON GRAND PUBLIC Division will be guaranteed payment of full wages during attendance of sessions of the European Committee.

Participants' names must be communicated to THOMSON GRAND PUBLIC at least two weeks before each meeting.
One of the two annual meetings must precede the annual session of the European Branch Committee.

IV-Competence
The Liaison Committee shall be informed of the economic, industrial and trading activities of THOMSON GRAND PUBLIC.
It will be informed, prior to the implementation, of major structural, industrial and trading modifications and changes in the economic and legal organisation of THOMSON GRAND PUBLIC.
It will be informed of measures taken and planned for adapting the organisation and workforce to technological change as well as adapting employees' skills in the light of employment problems.
The members of the Liaison Committee may express opinions, in the light of the information supplied, on all the areas defined above.
V — The EMF is to have access to the documents transmitted to the European Branch Committee.
It undertakes to respect the confidential or secret nature of these documents, as the case may be, *vis-à-vis* third parties.
VI — This protocol is concluded, on an experimental basis, for a period of two years as from 1st January 1986. The parties shall meet in the three months preceding its expiration in order to decide whether or not to renew these provisions.

PARIS
7th October 1985

EUROPEAN METAL WORKERS' FEDERATION	THOMSON GRAND PUBLIC
represented by Hubert THIERRON	represented by Jean-Jacques PEUCH-LESTRADE

FULC IG METALL CFDT CGT-FO UGT

The European Branch Committee

Considering the European character of the activities of the THOMSON GRAND PUBLIC Division, the signatories agree to set up a European Branch Committee, which is a new institution that must not lead to a diminution of the role of the French Branch Committee resulting from the agreement of 28th February 1984 signed with the representative French trade union organisations at THOMSON GRAND PUBLIC Division level.
This body must provide information for representatives of personnel

employed in the THOMSON GRAND PUBLIC Division, at European level, on its economic, industrial and trading situation.

I-Composition

- The Managing Director of the firm THOMSON GRAND PUBLIC or his representative, together with the managers concerned.
- 26 employee representatives appointed by the representative trade union organisations in France, Italy and Spain, at the Division level, from among the elected members of the Works Committees or Councils of subsidiaries of THOMSON GRAND PUBLIC and, in the case of the Federal Republic of Germany, by the Central Works Councils or, failing this, by the Works Councils.

II-Allocation of seats

In order to counter any disparities that may result from strict application of the rule of proportional representation in relation to the number of employees, each country will be represented, *a priori*, by 2 employee representatives.

Allocation of the other seats will be in proportion to the number of employees in the Division in the four European countries concerned, ie currently France, Germany, Italy and Spain.

On the basis of the total workforce as at 30th June 1985, employees of subsidiaries are to be represented as follows:

- French subsidiaries are represented by 13 members
- German subsidiaries are represented by 8 members
- Italian subsidiaries are represented by 3 members
- Spanish subsidiaries are represented by 2 members

The employee representatives of each country will be appointed, as laid down in paragraph 1, in accordance with the number of elected council members, as per the tables annexed to this protocol.

III-Procedure

The Branch Committee will meet once per year and will be convened by the management of THOMSON GRAND PUBLIC.

An *ad hoc* Committee may be constituted in respect of each problem liable to modify the industrial and trading position of the Division at European level. At its first meeting, the European Branch Committee will determine all details regarding the setting-up and operation of the *ad hoc* Committees.

The meeting costs (room and interpretation, as well as the accommodation and travel expenses incurred in respect of attendance of this meeting) will be met by THOMSON GRAND PUBLIC.

Employee representatives will be guaranteed payment of full wages for the duration of the meeting.

The names of the members of the European Branch Committee will be communicated to THOMSON GRAND PUBLIC by the appropriate bodies as per paragraph I before 31st December 1985.

The members of the European Branch Committee shall hold office for a period of two years.
During the two-year period of office, no other appointment may be made except in the following cases:

- Departure from the company or Division
- Change in trade union affiliation
- Loss of seat on a Works Committee or (Central) Works Council
- For the Federal Republic of Germany: Removal from appointed post by the Central Works Council or, failing this, the Works Council following the said Council's declared loss of confidence.

IV-Competence
The European Branch Committee will be informed of the Division's economic, industrial and trading activities in Europe and of the measures taken and planned for adapting personnel of subsidiaries in the countries concerned to technological change and adapting their skills in the light of employment problems.
The European Branch Committee will be informed, prior to implementation, of all major structural and industrial changes provided the decision is taken at Divisional level.
The European Branch Committee will be informed of economic and legal organisational changes in the Division (acquisition or transfer of subsidiaries).

V — The present protocol is concluded, on an experimental basis, for a period of two years as from 1st January 1986. The parties will meet in the three months preceding its expiration in order to decide whether or not to renew these provisions.

PARIS
7th October 1985

French trade union organisations
CFDT
CGC
CGT
CGT-FO

For and on behalf of the firm
THOMSON GRAND PUBLIC
Jean-Jacques PEUCH-LESTRADE

German Works Council or Central Works Council members

GBR NEWEK
GBR DEWEK
GBR SABA

GBR TELEFUNKEN
GBR DAGFU
GBR NORDMENDE

Italian trade union organisations
FULC

Spanish trade union organisations
UGT
CGOO
European Metalworkers' Federation

Appendix 4 Opinions from the Val Duchesse Talks

Joint Opinion of the Social Partners on the Cooperative Growth Strategy for More Employment

An in-depth exchange of views on the economic situation and employment in the Community was held at the meetings of the Macroeconomics Working Group (set up after the meeting between UNICE, CEEP and ETUC with the Commission on 12 November 1985), and the Commission's 1986–87 Annual Economic Report was discussed.

UNICE, CEEP and ETUC confirm their agreement on the basic principles of the Community's cooperative growth strategy for more employment and support the general thrust of the economic policy by the Commission in its 1986–87 Annual Economic Report.

They call on the governments of the member states to make a greater effort to ensure that the cooperative strategy is effectively implemented and declare their willingness to cooperate.

Full or broad agreement was reached on the following points:

1. In spite of the progress made on the employment front, unemployment is still too high. Unless additional efforts are made, it will not fall sufficiently in the medium term. The aim in implementing the cooperative growth strategy is to bring about a significant and lasting reduction in unemployment over a period of several years. In order to do this, more jobs must be created through increased investment based on improved business profitability and reinforcing the competitiveness of the European economy. Public investment also has an important role to play in this respect, without jeopardising the medium-term consolidation of public finance.
2. The creation of durable jobs will be threatened if inflation rates are not kept low. A stable financial environment encourages the propensity to invest. Monetary and budgetary policies should be managed in such a way as to ensure that inflation rates remain low or continue to fall. The social partners also share some responsibility for containing inflation.
3. Real interest rates should fall further, with account being taken of the world economic situation and savings behaviour. The liberalisation of

capital movements should help direct savings towards productive investment.

4. The internal market must be completed rapidly. This will make it possible to release considerable growth potential which will reinforce the positive effects which the implementation of the cooperative strategy will have on investment and growth. Completion of the internal market should be accompanied by taking account of social policy and by the development of structural policies to strengthen the Community's economic and social cohesion as it is defined in the Single European Act.
5. Research and development must be promoted so that the Community maintains or regains its technological competitiveness, particularly in 'high-tech' sectors. The Community should also encourage the implementation of the major mobilising programmes which are such as to promote growth and employment.
6. Improving the level of skills in the labour force and vocational retraining are important elements in developing employment and the competitiveness of the European economy. Training costs represent an investment. Employees at every level should be encouraged to take training courses.
7. The freedom of the world trade should be maintained and developed within the framework of GATT. The Community has a special responsibility in this respect. Generally, an effort must be made to continue to combat protectionist trends, unfair practices and escalating subsidies, the effect of which is to distort the conditions of competition. In certain cases, temporary bilateral or multilateral agreements could help to overcome specific problems.
8. In the framework of the cooperative strategy, moderate growth of real per capita wage costs below productivity gains should be maintained for some time to come in the countries in which it is already practised, and it should be applied in the other countries. But the other elements of the strategy must be implemented simultaneously. This will make an important contribution to improving business profitability and competitiveness as well as speeding up the implementation of job-creating investment. It is important here to highlight the link that exists between the moderation of wage costs — factor for increased profitability — and higher employment.
9. Appropriate tax measures, the development of new forms of financing, and easier access to risk capital can also strengthen investment and employment, notably in small and medium-sized firms.
10. Public investment and infrastructure investment have suffered under the process of budgetary consolidation, and there is at present some leeway to be made up here. Stronger expansion of such investment will make an important contribution, on both the supply and the demand sides, to achieving higher and sustained growth. Such investment should be regarded not as a way of compensating for the lack of private investment, but as complementary investment undertaken in the

general interest. Its financing could be achieved in the framework of a healthy budgetary policy through the restructuring of budgets and through the use of budgetary headroom that already exists or will be created by the growth process; furthermore, in a number of major instances, reliance on private financing seems possible and desirable. In this connection, the following distinctions were made:

(a) public investment or infrastructure investment which is profitable in itself but which, without public initiatives, would not be carried out at the appropriate time because of its scale or because of its long pay-off period (for example, the Channel tunnel and the high-speed-train link between Paris, Brussels and Cologne); in the case of this type of investment, private financing can most easily be envisaged;

(b) public investment or infrastructure investment which is economically profitable in overall terms because it represents a precondition for private investment or for the development of certain countries or regions; in the case of this type of investment, on the basis of rigorous economic calculation, certain forms of cofinancing by the private sector can be examined;

(c) public investment intended to meet justified public or social needs; its profitability must not be seen solely in economic terms; deciding on the priority projects in this area is also a matter of political judgement: cofinancing by the private sector is more difficult to envisage, but not to be ruled out in all cases.

UNICE, CEEP AND ETUC are convinced that dialogue is an important element in the effective implementation of the Community's cooperative growth strategy for more employment. They are prepared to continue the dialogue, especially on questions not yet resolved (eg reduction in government spending and in taxes and social security contributions, the adaptability of financial, commercial and labour markets, revision of certain regulations, more flexible wage formation, reorganisation and duration of working time, etc).

Brussels, 6 November 1986.

Joint Opinion of the Val Duchesse New Technologies Working Party

The joint opinion adopted at the March 6 meeting of the working party on 'Social Dialogue and the New Technologies' (see European Report No 1297), which was convened by the European Commission following the November 12, 1985 meeting at the Val Duchesse Chateau in Brussels between representatives of the Union of European Community Industries (UNICE), the European Centre of Public Enterprises (CEEP) and the

European Trade Union Confederation (ETUC), has now been made available in English. The full text of the opinion is reproduced below:

(A) Training and motivation

The participants in this group issued the following joint opinion concerning the part of their work related to training and motivation:

1. They took the view that the process of introducing new technologies would be economically more viable and socially more acceptable if accompanied, among other things, by effective training and greater motivation for both workers and managerial staff, factors which, in their view, constitute a genuine investment.
   To this end, every member of the staff of the firm, at all levels of responsibility, should be encouraged to make the necessary efforts at adaptation and training, also through personal commitment.
2. They also stressed that vocational training — comprising basic training, in-service training and retraining — should be able to satisfy the demands of workers, firms, the economy in general and of the internal market in particular. From this point of view and in the spirit of this opinion, the work carried out by the Commission and by CEDEFOP on the development of training systems and their comparability needs the active support of both sides of industry and of the Governments. A system for the mutual recognition of qualifications should be rapidly introduced at European level.
3. They point out that responsibility for basic training, whether provided by the education systems or the basic training systems, lies with the public authorities.[1] However, in order to ensure greater consistency between training and the requirements of the economy and of firms and workers, the authorities should consult and involve the social partners more than they do at present.
4. With a view to the adaptation of the training systems, they consider that the social partners must actively contribute towards the transition of young people from school to working life, more particularly by developing the Community programme of pilot projects. In this context, they stress the need to reorganise the education systems so as to make them more efficient — from basic training to training in advanced skills — and promote greater versatility and the acquisition of basic skills required for the transition of young people to adult working life. Priority should be attached to the development of a continuous process of guidance and counselling as well as to the training of trainers and to the methods of training needed in order to meet these requirements.
5. They also consider that in-service training should enable employees to adapt swiftly and continuously to structural changes in the firm, and that

[1] Unless provided by the firms themselves.

the costs of such training should be borne primarily by the firm itself. Information and consultation of the workforce or, depending on national practice, of its representatives, on training programmes carried out by the undertaking, would help to increase employees' motivation by also improving their understanding of the changes facing the firm.[1]

6. They stress that retraining measures must enable employees to find work or another job — as set out in paragraph 2 above — either in the same firm or elsewhere. It will, in principle, be the firm within which the worker continues to be employed with different skills which will have to bear the cost of these measures. However, at the same time, they emphasised that the economic and social value of a retraining policy implies that public vocational training bodies should play a part so as to ensure a proper distribution of the costs, and a better utilisation of resources. By contrast, the burden of retraining workers who no longer continue to be employed by the original firm will have to be borne by the public authorities or the firm which recruits them.
7. They also took the view that in-service training and retraining would be more effective if backed up by a policy designed to improve the forecasting of trends as regards skills and employment, particularly at regional and local level, so as to promote convergence between the respective aims of training and employment.
8. As regards the implementation of a vocational training policy for small and medium-sized enterprises, a more detailed study should be made of the ways and means by which the specific characteristics of these undertakings could be accommodated.
9. Special attention should be devoted to unskilled first job seekers, particularly as concerns people under 25 years of age and women.

(B) Information and consultation

Acknowledging the need to master and manage the changes resulting from the process of industrial transformation now in progress, so as to make them effective and socially acceptable, the members of the working party issued the following joint opinion on that part of their work which relates to information and consultation in connection with the introduction of new technologies in firms.

1. To clarify what follows, 'Information and Consultation' must be understood as applying to workers and/or their representatives, in accordance with the laws, collective agreements and practices in force in the countries of the Community.
2. The participants recognised the need to make use of the economic and social potential offered by technological innovation in order to enhance the competitiveness of European firms and strengthen economic

[1] CONFINDUSTRIA refers here to the arrangements arising out of collective agreements drawn up in Italy.

growth, thus creating one of the necessary conditions for better employment and, taking particular account of progress in the field of ergonomics, for improved working conditions.

3. The participants stress the need to motivate the staff at all levels of responsibility in firms and to develop their aptitude to change, among other ways by means of good information and consultation practices.

   They consider that such motivation will be all the higher if all the staff are in a position to understand the economic and social need for structural and technological change and the potential which such change offers to firms and to the workforce.

4. The participants note that, in most countries of the Community and also in many industrial sectors, there exist various forms of information and consultation procedures and negotiating practices. While accepting the diversity of the existing procedures, they consider that best use should be made of the existing procedures.

5. Both sides take the view that, when technological changes which imply major consequences for the workforce are introduced in the firm, workers and/or their representatives should be informed and consulted in accordance with the laws, agreements and practices in force in the Community countries. This information and consultation must be timely.

   In this context:

   - Information means the action of providing the workers and/or their representatives, at the level concerned, with relevant details of such changes, so as to enlighten them as to the firm's choices and the implications for the workforce;
   - consultation of the workers and/or their representatives, at the level concerned, means the action of gathering opinions and possible suggestions concerning the implications of such changes for the firm's workforce, more particularly as regards the effects on their employment and their working conditions.

6. Both sides consider that information and consultation may, in certain circumstances, require an obligation to observe secrecy or confidentiality in order to prevent any damage to the firm.

   The conditions relating to such confidentiality and the power to withhold the secret or confidential information, as also the need to provide timely information concerning major changes in the terms of employment and working conditions of the staff concerned fall within the scope of the laws, agreements and practices in force in the countries of the Community.

7. Both sides state that information and consultation must facilitate and should not impede the introduction of new technology, the final decisions being exclusively the responsiblity of the employer or of the decision-making bodies of the firm. It is understood that this prerogative does not exclude the possibility of negotiation where the parties take a decision to that effect.

8. In order to improve understanding of the new technologies, promote

the acquisition of new skills and enhance adaptability, both sides express the wish that appropriate training for both employers and workers be developed.

In this connection, both sides express the wish that the Commission develop ways and means of contributing to this process.

9. Despite their differences as to the appropriateness of resorting to Community legal instruments, both sides recognise that it is worthwhile encouraging the development of information and consultation practices in matters relating to the introduction of new technologies in the countries of the Community.
10. Furthermore, both sides note that, on the basis of a variety of practices, adaptability and flexibility are developing throughout the Community. To this end, the two sides confirm their readiness to continue the social dialogue on the implications of the introduction of the new technologies.

References

Baldry C *et al* (1984) 'Multinational closure and the case of Massey Ferguson, Kilmarnock', *Industrial Relations Journal*, **15** No a 1984, pp 17–27.

Baranouin B (1986) *The European Labour Movement and European Integration*, Frances Pinter, London.

Barratt-Brown M (1977) *Working class internationalism*, No 33, pp 23–28, Spokesman, Nottingham.

Beretta D (1987) *Social Aspects of the Internal Market*, Brussels Economic and Social Committee Information Report No 134.

Blanpain R (1983) *The Vredeling Proposal: information and consultation of employers in multinational enterprises*, Deventer, Boston.

Blanpain R *et al* (1984) *Workers' Participation in the European Communities*, Kluwer, Deventer.

Blanpain R (ed) (1985) *Comparative Labour Law and Industrial Relations*, Kluwer, Deventer.

Boyer R (1988) *In Search of Labour Market Flexibility: European Economies in Transition*, Clarendon Press, Oxford.

Brewster C and Teague P (1989) *European Social Policy and the United Kingdom*, Institute of Personnel Management, London.

CBI, (1986) *The European Community and Social Engineering*, London.

Coates D (ed) (1986) *Joint Action for Jobs*, Spokesman, Nottingham.

Coates D and Topham T (1986) *Trade Unions and Politics*, Basil Blackwell, Oxford.

Collins D (1975) *The European Communities: The Social Policy of the First Phase*, Martin Robertson, London.

Collins D (1982) 'The Impact of Social Policy in the United Kingdom' in A Al-Algra (ed) *Britain in the European Community: The Way Forward*, Macmillan, London.

Commission of the European Community (1974) 'The Social Action Programme', *Bulletin of the European Community*, No 10, pp 370–380.

– (1978) *Interest Group Representation in the European Community*, Brussels, Document.

– (1987a) 'Youth Training in the European Community', *Social Europe*, Supplement No 3.

– (1987b) *Internal and External Adaption of Firms in relation to Employment*, Com (87) 229 Final.

– (1987c) *Report on the Follow to the Council Resolution of 22nd December on an Action Programme for Employment Growth*, Com (87) 303 Final.

– (1987d) *Report on Social Developments*, Brussels, Document.

– (1987e) *Programme Concerning Safety, Hygiene and Health at Work*, Com (87) 229 Final.

– (1988) *The Social Dimension to the Internal Market*, Social Europe Special Edition, No 3.

Community Markets (1983) 'US Firms oppose Vredeling', April, No 4, *Financial Times*, London.

Community Markets (1983) 'Centre Stage for Vredeling', July, No 8, *Financial Times*, London.

Cox A (1988) 'The Old and New Testaments of Corporatism: Is it a Political Form or a Method of Policy-making', *Political Studies* No 3.

Cripps L (1987) 'The Social Policy of the European Community', *Social Europe* No 1, pp 51–57.

Crouch C and Pizzorno A (ed) (1978) *The Resurgence of Class Conflict in Western Europe since 1968*, Macmillan, London.

Crouch C (1986) 'Conservative industrial relations policy: towards labour exclusion', in O Jacobi *et al* (ed) *Economic Crisis, Trade Unions and the State*, Croom Helm, London.

Crouch C (1986) 'Future prospects for the trade unions in western Europe', *The Political Quarterly*, **57** No 1, pp 5–18.

Danses M (1985) 'The Protection of Fundamental Rights in the Community Legal Order', *European Law Review* **10** No 6, 1985, pp 398–421.

Delores J (1986) 'The Work Programme of the European Commission', Speech to the European Parliament, February.

Delores J (1988) 'L'espace Sociale', Speech to the ETUC Congress, Stockholm, March.

Department of Employment (1986), *Action Programme for Employment Growth*, HMSO, London.

Docksey C (1985) 'Employee information and consultation rights in the Member States of European Community' *Comparative Labour Law Journal* No 2, pp 32–69.

Docksey C (1988) 'The Enforcement of Community Law on Equality at the National level', *Social Europe* No 1, pp 9–13.

Eaben A J (1979) 'The Direct Effect of EEC Directives', *International and Comparative Law Quarterly* No 4, pp 319–353.

Edwards R (ed) (1986) *Trade Unions in Crisis and Beyond*, Auburn House Publishing Company, Dover, Massachusetts.

Engineering Employers Federation (1984) European Employment Law, Political Statement, London.

ETUC (1979) Interview with H Vetter, Press Release, 16 April.

ETUC (1982) *European Initiatives on Information and Consultation for Workers*, Brussels, Document.

ETUC (1987) *The Social Dimension to the Internal Market Programme*, Press Release.

European Parliament (1986) *The European Social Area*, Working Document No A2–141/86.

Fogarty M (1975) *Work and Industrial Relations in the European Community*, PEP European Series No 24, London.

Fredman F (1989 forthcoming) *The Future of European Labour Law*, Macmillan, London.

Giersch H (1987) *Eurosclerosis*, Kiel Discussion Papers, No 112.

Glassen J and McGee T (1983) *EEC Aid and local authorities — Some Research Findings — an Interim Report*, Oxford Polytechnic, Oxford.

Gourevitch P *et al* (1984) *Unions, Change and Crisis*, Allen and Unwin, London.

Grahl J and Teague P (1989a) 'The Costs of Neo Liberal Europe', *New Left Review*, March/April.

Grahl J and Teague P (1989b) 'European Community Social Policy: Present Scope and Future Direction', *Journal of European Integration*.

Grahl J and Teague P (1989c) *The Big Market: European Economic Cooperation in the 1990s*, Lawrence and Wishart, London.

Haas E (1958) *The Uniting of Europe*, Stanford University Press, California.

Hansenne A (1987) 'Does Europe want Flexibility through Deregulation', *Social and Labour Bulletin* No 4, pp 1–8.

Haworth N and Ramsey H (1987) 'Labour and Management in the World Market: The Plot Thickens', in D Judge and T Dickens *The Politics of Closure*, Macmillan, Basingstoke.
Hayward J (1980) *Trade Unions and Politics in Western Europe*, Frank Cass, London.
Hayward J (1986) *The State and the Market Economy*, Wheatsheaf Books, London.
Health and Safety Commission (1987) Submission to the House of Commons Select Committee on Employment, 2 April.
Hepple B (1977) 'Community measures for the protection of workers against dismissals', *Common Market Law Review* No 14, pp 839–849.
– (1982) 'The Transfer of Undertakings (Protection of Employment Regulations)' *Industrial Law Journal* No 1, pp 29–42.
– (1983) 'Harmonization of Labour Law in the European Communities' in *Essays for Clive Schmitthoff*, Abingdon, London.
– (1987) 'The Crisis in EC Labour Law,' *Industrial Law Journal* **16** No 12, pp 3–16.
Holland M (1985) 'The EEC Code for South Africa', *World Today*, **41** No 1, pp 12–15.
Hoskyns C (1987) 'Women, European Law and International Politics, *International Journal of the Sociology of Law*', November, pp 33–51.
House of Lords Select Committee on the European Communities, Voluntary (1982) *Part-Time Work*, 18th Report 1982.
House of Lords Select Committee on the European Communities, (1985) *Parental Leave and Leave for Family Reasons*, 3rd Report, HMSO, London.
Hume J (1988) Submission to the House of Lords Select Committee on the European Communities on the Reform of the Structural Funds, Session 1987–1988, 14th Report.
Hurwitz L (1988) *The European Community and the Management of International Cooperation*, Greenwood Press, New York.
Income Data Services (1984) *The Transfer of Undertakings Regulations*, London.
Johnson E (1986) 'EC Structural Funds and Deindustrialization', in C Mellows, *Promoting local authorities in the European Community*, IULA, London.
Kirchner E (1978) *Trade Unions as Pressure Groups in the European Community*, Gower, Aldershot.
– (1980) *Interest Groups in the European Community*, Gower, Aldershot.
– (1983) *Public Service Unions and the European Community*, Gower, Aldershot.
Krasner S D (ed) (1983), *International Regimes*, Cornell University Press, New York.
Landau E (1985) *The Rights of Working Women in the European Community*, European Perspective Series, Brussels.
Lange P *et al* (1982), *Unions, Crisis and Change*, Allen and Unwin, London.
Lee J (1987) 'The UK Government's view of EC Social Policy', speech to the Annual Conference of the Institute of Personnel Management.
Leenan A (1986) 'Equal Treatment of Male and Female Employees under European Community Law', *Legal Issues of European Integration*, No 1, pp 91–115.
Levinson C (1972) *International Trade Unionism*, Allen and Unwin, London.
Lindbeck A (1985) 'What is Wrong with the West European Economies', *World Economy*, **8** No 2, pp 153–170.
Lipietz A (1988) 'L'Europe dernier recours pour une relance mondiale', *Le Monde Diplomatique*, May.
Lipietz A and Leborgne D (1988) 'L'Apres Fordisme et son espace', *Les Temps Modernes*, April.
Lodge J (1978) 'Giving the Community a Human Face: the attempt to construct a European Social Policy', *British Review of International Affairs*, March, pp 57–71.

Lodge J (1986) 'The Single European Act: Towards a Dynamism?' *Journal of Common Market Studies*, March, pp 57–71.

McCrudden C (ed) (1987) *Women, Employment and European Equality Law*, Eclipse Publications, London.

Madelin A (1988) 'Creating a Single European Market II: A French View', *World Today*, March.

Mazey S (1988) 'European Community Equal Opportunities Policies: The Limits to Legislation', *Journal of Common Market Studies*, September, pp 352–374.

Morley J (1982) Oral Evidence to the House of Commons Select Committee on the European Community, Voluntary Part-Time Work, 19th Report, HMSO, London.

National Association of Pension Funds (1987) Submission to the House of Lords Selected Committee on the European Communities on Social Security in the European Community, Session 1987–88, 3rd Report 1986.

Northrup H and Rowan R (1977) 'Multinational union-management consultation: the European experience', *International Labour Review*, No 5, pp 153–170.

Northrup H *et al* (1988) 'Multinational union-management consultation in Europe: Resurgence in the 1980s?', *International Labour Review*, No 5, pp 3–21.

Offe C (1987) 'Challenging the boundaries of institutional politics: social movements since the 1960s', in C Mair (ed) *Changing Boundaries of the Political*, Cambridge University Press, New York.

Padoa-Schioppa T *et al* (1987) *Efficiency, Stability and Efficiency: A Strategy for the Evolution of the Economic System of the European Community*, Oxford University Press, Oxford.

Palmer J (1987) *Europe without America*, Oxford University Press, Oxford.

Pescatore P (1983) 'The Doctrine of Direct Effect: An Infant Disease', *European Law Review*, **8** No 3, pp 155–179.

Pipkorn J (1977) 'Comparative Labour Law in the Harmonization of Social Standards in the European Community', *Comparative Labor Law*, **12** No 1.

Pipkorn J (1984) 'Employee participation in the European Community: progress and pitfalls', in B Wilpert and A Sorge (ed) *International Perspectives on Organisational Democracy*, John Wiley & Sons, Chichester.

Rebhan H (1985) 'Trade Unions and Multinational Collective Bargaining', Speech given to a Financial Times/IRM Conference on Transnational companies in the World Economy.

Robbins B (1986) 'The Social Policies of the European Community', *Personnel Management* March, pp 32–39.

Roberts B (1971) 'The European Community as an Industrial Relations System', *Comparative Labour Law*, No 3, pp 17–24.

Roberts B and Liebhieberg R (1976) 'The European Trade Union Confederation: Influence of Regionalism, Detente and the Multinationals', *British Journal of Industrial Relations*, **14** No 3, pp 261–274.

Rubenstein M (1984) *Equal Pay for Work of Equal Value*, Macmillan, London.

Rubenstein M (1987) 'The Equal Treatment Directive and UK Law', in C McCrudden (ed) *Women, Employment and European Equality Law*, Eclipse Publications, London.

Ryan P R (1984) 'The New Training Initiative: An Assessment', *Lloyds Bank Review*, March, pp 21–33.

Sargent J (1986) 'The Theory of Corporatism and the European Community', in W Grant *The Political Economy of Corporatism*, Macmillan, London.

Sargent J (1987) 'Business Organisations in the European Community', in W Grant with J Sargent, *Business and Politics*, Macmillan, Basingstoke.

Schmitter P (1969) 'A Revised Theory of Regional Integration', *International Organisation*, No 4, pp 836–869.
Shanks M (1977) 'The Social Policy of the European Communities' *Common Market Law Review* No 14, pp 370–386.
Shaw B (1988) Submission to the House of Lords Select committee on the European Communities, on the Reform of the Structural Funds, Session 1987–88, 14th Report.
Taylor P (1983) *The Limits of European Integration*, Croom Helm, London.
Taylor P (1989 forthcoming) 'European Integration in the 1980s: the new dynamics' in J Lodge *The European Community in the 1990s*, Macmillan, London.
Teague P (1984) *Labour and Europe: The response of British trade unions to membership of the European Community*, Unpublished PhD thesis, University of London.
Teague P (1985) The Alternative Economic Strategy: A Time to European, *Capital and Class* No 25 pp 43–69.
Teague P (1988) *The Labour Market Policies of the European Community*, Cranfield: Cranfield Human Resources Monograph Series, No 4.
Teague P (1989a) 'Trade Unions and Extra-National Industrial Policies: A case-study of the NUM and ISTC in the European Community', *Economic and Industrial Democracy*, Cranfield, June.
Teague P (1989b) 'The British TUC and the European Community, Millenium, *Journal of International Relations*, March.
Trades Union Congress (1975) Annual Report, London.
Treu T (1986) 'Equal Pay and Comparable Work: A View from Europe' *Comparative Labour Law Journal* No 8, pp 2–19.
Tyszkiewicz Z (1986) 'The achievement of the internal market by 1992 and the European Social Space: the employers view', Speech given to the Management Centre of Europe.
Ulman L (1975) Multinational Unionism: Incentives, Barriers and Alternatives, *Industrial Relations*, No 12, pp 1–31.
Vandamme J (1984) *Pou une nouvelle politique social en Europe*, Economica, Paris.
Wainwright H (1987) A *Taste of Power: the politics of local economies*, Verso, London.
Wallace W (1984) 'The European Community: More than a Regime less than a Federation', in W Wallace *et al* (ed) *Policy-making in the European Community*, John Wiley & Sons, Chichester.
Wallace W and Hodges M (1981) *Economic Divergence in the European Community*, Macmillan, London.
Welsh M (1987) *Labour Market Policy in the European Community: The British Presidency of 1986*, Royal Institute of International Affairs, Discussion Paper No 4, London.
Windmuller J P (1976) 'European Regionalism: A New Factor in International Labour', *Industrial Relations Journal*, 7 No 2, pp 36–45.
Wyatt D (1984) 'The Direct Effect of Community Social Law — not Forgetting Directives', *European Law Review* No 4, pp 241–248.

List of Acronyms

ACAS	Advisory Conciliation and Arbitration Service
BGs	Berufsgenossenschaften
CBI	Confederation of British Industry
CEC	Commission of the European Community
CEDEFOP	European Centre for the Development of Vocational Training
DGV	Directorate of Social Affairs, Employment and Education
ECU	European Currency Unit
EEF	Engineering Employers Federation
EMF	European Metalworkers Federation
EOC	Equal Opportunities Commission
ERDF	European Regional Fund
ETUC	European Trade Union Confederation
FEOGA	European Agricultural Guideline and Guarantee Fund
GAs	Gewerbeaufsicht
HSE	Health and Safety Executive
ILO	International Labour Organisation
IMF	International Metalworkers Federation
MSC	Manpower Services Commission
OECD	Organisation of Economic Cooperation and Development
SEA	Single European Act
SEDOC	The European System for the International Clearing of Vacancies and Applications for Employment
SETE	Services Entérieure du Travail et de l'Emploi
TUC	Trades Union Congress
UNICE	Union of Industrial and Employers Confederations of Europe

Index